TABLE OF CONTENTS

Preface v

Introduction vii

Chapter One: My Seven-Step Journey 5

Chapter Two: "How To" Move On Beyond Transformation 23

Chapter Three: "How To" Walk In The Spirit of God 33

Chapter Four: "How To" Avoid The Multiplicity Factor 67

Chapter Five: "How To" Master Spiritual Self-Defense 70

Chapter Six: "How To" Escape The Reality of Hell 98

Chapter Seven: "How To" Spot Heresy in the Church 117

Chapter Eight: "How To" Live Out Your Divine Destiny 137

Conclusion 168

Selected Christian Poetry By John Marinelli, The Author 171

About The Author 193

REALITY SQUARED

*HOW TO ATTAIN AND ENJOY
THE REALITY OF GOD*

JOHN MARINELLI

Reality Squared: How to Attain and Enjoy the Reality of God
Copyright © 2024 by Rev. John Marinelli. All rights are reserved.

No portion of this book may be reproduced without the author's written consent. Respond to johnmarinelli@embarqmail.com.

1st edition February 2024.
Rev. John Marinelli
P.O. 831413
Ocala FL 34483

Print ISBN: 979-8-8690-9061-4
eBook ISBN: 979-8-8690-9062-1

PREFACE

"Reality Squared" is a Biblical teaching on *"How To"* attain and enjoy the reality of God. It is a search for the Biblical pathway into the presence of God. It begins with an in-depth Bible study to discover all there is to know.

The reader of this book will learn how to be transformed from a life of carnality, where sadness, depression, and immorality reign into the *"Will of God"* in real-time. If done seriously, the study will transform the mind into an abundance of life where love, joy, peace, and other attributes of God flow freely.

I titled this book: "Reality Squared" because I felt there is more than just man's reality. God is far above man's existence, and he has his own separate reality. It is this reality that my teaching is all about. Thus, the title, "Reality Squared."

I wrote this teaching because of my quest to be more like Jesus and less like my liberal society. I knew there must be more to living than what I was experiencing. I also believed that the answer was in the scriptures. The study of the scriptures offered a pathway to personal freedom from an inward sin nature, the outward evil attacks of Satan, and the expectations of non-Christian individuals around me. This is my quest that began over 60 years ago.

INTRODUCTION

What is reality? The dictionary says this about that:

re·al·i·ty [rēˈalədē] NOUN

- a thing that is actually experienced or seen, especially when this is grim or problematic: (*the harsh realities of life in a farming community" · "the law ignores the reality of the situation"*)

SIMILAR: fact- actuality- truth- verity

- a thing that exists in fact, having previously only existed in one's mind: *("the paperless office may yet become a reality")*
- the state or quality of having existence or substance: *("youth, when death has no reality")*

The Biblical definition of reality…That reality is the way things really are. Reality is what it is because God declared it to be so and made it so. God is the author, source, determiner, governor, arbiter, ultimate standard, and final judge of all truth. The Bible assumes a fundamental duality in reality, with an irreducible ontological interval between God and everything else.(Ontological = relating to the branch of metaphysics dealing with the nature of being)

Reality can be defined in a way that links it to worldviews or parts of them. (conceptual frameworks): **Reality is the totality of all things**, structures (actual and conceptual), events (past and present) and phenomena, whether observable or not.

Reality is the independent nature and existence of everything knowable, whether it is knowable by logical inference, empirical observation, or some other form of experience. The common misconception is that reality and truth convey the same meaning, but that is not accurate.

Reality is the sum or aggregate of all that is real or existent within the universe, as opposed to that which is only imaginary, nonexistent or nonactual. In physical terms, reality is the totality of a system known and unknown.

In today's world, people have reduced reality to a point of view**.** It is *a perspective or way of thinking.* It drives us to be a certain way and do things that shape our destiny. My reality can be very different from yours because you may think along different lines than I do. That's why there are liberal thinkers and conservative thinkers that clash constantly in the political arena and on social platforms. That's why there are gays and straights. That's why women think differently than men. Everyone has his or her own reality or view of life that they live out in different lifestyles. However, beyond all of this is the "Reality of God."

I asked a few friends to explain reality to me from their viewpoint.

One friend said that reality was determined by how much money you have which would shape the lifestyle in which you would live. Money equals a lavish lifestyle and ease. Poverty would create a lifestyle of suffering and struggle. The "Haves" and the "Have-nots." This was his point of view concerning reality. (Remember, the actual definition of reality is: **"The totality of all things"**, so, my 1st friend is not correct because money and lifestyle does not make up true reality.

Another friend believed that childhood experiences shape one's reality, determining whether they become a positive or negative adult. This was the foundation of his lifestyle. (Again, this answer, that everybody has different experiences, and that is their reality, would negate an absolute. **"The totality of all things" is an absolute**,)

Yet another friend said that their reality was the sum total of their education, which made them what they are today. (This too is incorrect because reality is *the total of everything that exists*, not everything that is learned.)

Then I talked to one more friend that said reality to him was an ever-changing flow of thoughts that took him into depression and/or other negative feelings from which he could not escape. This was his reality. (This too is incorrect because all thoughts are not the same for every individual. They may shape one's destiny, but they are not *the total of everything that exists*.)

Finally, I spoke with a phycologist friend that defined reality as "Now." He said the past was gone, and the future has yet to be determined. All that exists is this very moment, and that is reality. (We are indeed living in the moment, but our moment does not cover all that is actual and existing everywhere else. We may not see the billions of people on earth, but they are actual, real, and existing just the same. Plus, a building that was real in the past may still be today, even though it is not in our current moment. Thus, he too is mistaken.)

So, I then planned my theory of reality. Based upon my past education and Biblical knowledge, plus my personal Christianity, I reasoned that true reality had to be realized on a spiritual level, not physical. I also reasoned that there were many realities in life that shape the lifestyles of folks in our society. There could be 7-billion realities on earth, one for every person. They are clashing with each other every day for supremacy. However, they all deal with reality from a personal perspective. They are, in fact, just a little piece of a bigger world view and not universal.

I investigated many different realities and found that, for the most part, they were not based on any Biblical truth. Instead, they were rooted in humanism, feel-good theories, and had a carnal nature. Even the world religions were Anti-Christ in their thinking with a reality that supported false gods and doctrines. *Reality should be that which is true, but often it is not. Instead, people present it as truth, but it is actually a false assumption.* (Jesus said, "Take heed therefore that the light which is in thee be not darkness.") Luke 11:35.

As I studied the scriptures, I discovered that there was a reality where God exists and is Lord over his creation. I also discovered that there was a pathway that would lead me into that reality which is different from what most other folks experience. I discovered I could see, feel, and know the presence of God in real time, day- by-day. I could actually live, and have my being in the *"Reality of God.*

My search revealed that man's reality was very different from God's reality. His reality is unseen, but nevertheless there. It is just as real, if not more real, than what man experiences. Everything in God's reality is true and purpose driven. In contrast, man's reality is filled with lies, deception, and fear, which influence his thoughts and shape his reality and subsequent lifestyle. Truth is not the basis for man's reality. Man has lost truth in his quest for self-identity. What is real is not a prerequisite. If it were, we would all be living in God's reality.

I am pleased to share my 60+ year journey with you, hoping you too can find yourself and live in a world that is ordered by God and blessed with his grace and love.

The Pathway to the Reality of God

There is a pathway that leads to the reality of God. This path is not clear, so as folks could readily see it and know where it goes. The pathway hides itself in plain sight, and only those who seek God can find it.

As we study, we will look at Romans, chapter twelve, with a look back at the end of chapter eleven. I will also add other supporting scriptures as relevant to my discussion.

Based on the material from Acts and the Corinthian epistles, we can clearly see that Paul wrote the Book of Romans from Corinth on his third missionary journey. Paul had never visited Rome; but after fulfilling his mission of mercy to Jerusalem, he hoped to go to Rome in route to Spain (Rom. 15:23-25). At any rate, the date of the book is probably 60 A.D.

At the end of chapter eleven, Paul said this, "For of him, and through him and to him, are all things: to whom be glory forever. Amen." (He speaks of Jesus)

The beginning of chapter twelve, Paul continued with a, "Therefore" said this, "I beseech you *therefore*, brethren, by the mercies of God, that ye present your bodies a living sacrifice, holy, acceptable unto God, which is your reasonable service and be not conformed to this world: but be ye transformed by the renewing of your mind, that ye may prove what is that good, and acceptable, and perfect, will of God." Romans 12:2

The reason or need for us to be transformed is so we can prove what is that good, and acceptable, and perfect will of God. Thus, knowing the perfect will of God is discernable, but not by worldly methods. It takes the Spirit of God to see into spiritual things. That's why Paul begs us to be transformed.

Paul is pleading with or (Beseeching) the Christians at Rome, based on 11:36, (Because all things are of him, through him and to him). 12:1 "Therefore, we, by the mercies of God, ought to present our bodies as a *living sacrifice* which is holy and acceptable unto God."

This action, although noteworthy, is difficult. Paul knew this and thus tells his believers that it will require a transformation from worldly to spiritual; from walking in darkness to walking in the light of God's love; from immorality to morality. Life as they knew it would have to change radically. Their thinking will have to become brand new.

The mind will have to be renewed.. So…to be transformed, we need to exchange our corrupt minds with the mind of Christ. We need to restore our minds to a condition of holiness. The problem is, we have never been in that holy mindset, so restoration is seemingly impossible because we do not know what that looks like…or do we?

The unsaved man is like Adam after he fell from God's grace. He is without God's indwelling Spirit (Breath of Life). He was separated from God and left to walk in spiritual darkness.

The saved man is like Jesus. He possesses the indwelling Spirit of the living God. (His Breadth of Life) He is privileged to hear God's voice, understand his logic, and be blessed by his wisdom. All of this came to man when he was "Born Again." John 3:16.

The invisible nature of God now shines in and through his children, who have been "Born Anew" by his Spirit. It's like a butterfly that once was a crawling, worm-like creature that experiences transformation and becomes a beautiful butterfly. This is a vivid picture of a, "New Creature". The old passed away, rather…was transformed into something entirely new.

We are buried into baptism with Christ and raised with him in newness of life. Colossians 2:12. Anyone who says they are alive in God and does not believe in the burial by baptism and a personal resurrection with Christ is deceived and probably not really saved.

Here is what Paul said to the Galatians: (Chapter Three) "O foolish Galatians, who hath bewitched you, that ye should not obey the truth, before whose eyes Jesus Christ hath been evidently set forth, crucified among you? This only would I learn of you, received ye the Spirit by the works of the law, or by the hearing of faith? Are ye so foolish? Having begun in the Spirit, are ye now made perfect by the flesh?" Galatians 3:1-35.

This is a prime example of a need to be renewed. They drifted away from spiritual things, returning to the things of the flesh. If you read on, you will discover that they had abandoned the concept of God's saving grace to trust in the Law of Moses as a spiritual guide for salvation. Paul said they were foolish. So…we now know that we are to be transformed and the way to accomplish that transformation is to renew our minds…to go back to the simplicity of the gospel and follow in the footsteps of Christ. Let me explain.

The world system of things… like Liberalism, Secularism, Gay Rights, Gender Reclassification, and other immoral posturing, has worn off on us.

The world's influence has led to a general lack of faith and a general falling away from the gospel of grace. They were once dedicated to God's will, not their own. He was the center of their lives and they found themselves in him, not in the things of this world. His mindset was what they sought and found in his lordship. They could see life from his perspective.

The pathway to the reality of God was through a renewal of their minds. It was the only way they could escape the sinful nature inside of them and attain and enjoy God's grace in real time.

So, we will embark on the same journey that the 1st century saints took to be transformed from "death unto life"; "darkness into light"; "lost to being saved" and from "sorrow into an abundance of joy." Our journey will take us into a renewal process that will deliver us into the reality of God.

CHAPTER ONE:
MY SEVEN-STEP JOURNEY

I began my search for the *"Reality of God"* by going on a spiritual seven-step journey, designed to open my eyes and teach my spirit about the things of God. My goal was to discover Biblical truths that would influence my thinking and guide my thought life.

If you take my seven-step spiritual journey in search of *"The Reality of God"* you may wish to keep a journal, jotting down your feelings and revelations from God as you move from step to step.

I suggest one day per step to absorb all the Biblical truth in that step. However, one day may not be enough. You may need one week or even more. Take all the time you need. The goal is to get God's Word in you so you can use it. The purpose is to establish a *"Godly Mindset"* that brings about a perspective that is pleasing and acceptable to God. The result is to renew your mind. So, let's look at the 1st of 7 steps in renewing your minds.

Remember, our goal is to move from man's flawed reality into God's perfect reality. This will require serious evaluation of those things we now look at as our reality. Some will have to go, while others can stay as the Spirit of the Lord shows us.

Step #1

Become A Living Sacrifice

Most of us get up each day, running away from life or trying to master it with all our energies. Paul tells us we are to present ourselves unto God as a **"Living *Sacrifice.*"** He further says that this action is reasonable, considering what Christ did for us. Romans 12:2.

Paul's admonition to sacrifice ourselves to God did not mean physical death. We were not to be burned on the altar, as the sacrifices were in ancient Israel. We were, however, to sacrifice the world we live in with all its evil and to deny ourselves any evil lifestyle associated with it. This is what is meant by a *living* sacrifice. We go on living, but not as we did before; in riotous living, drunkenness, immorality, adultery, and all the other deeds of the flesh spoken of in Galatians chapter five.

What does a living sacrifice look like in the practical sense?

The following verse (Romans 12:2) helps us to understand. We become a living sacrifice by not being conformed to this world. The world is defined for us in 1 John 2:15-16 *as the lust of the flesh, the lust of the eyes, and the pride of life.* All that the world has to offer can be reduced to these three things.

- **"The Lust of the Flesh"** includes everything that appeals to our appetites and involves excessive desires for food, drink, sex, and anything else that satisfies physical pleasures.
- **"The Lust of the Eyes"** mostly involves materialism, coveting whatever we see that we don't have, and envying those who have what we want.
- **"The Pride of Life"** is defined by any ambition for that which puffs us up and puts us on the throne of our own lives.

Our transformation away from this world happens as we renew our minds. We do this primarily through the power of God's Word. The Holy Spirit teaches us as we read the Bible and pray. This is the only power on earth that can transform us from worldliness to true spirituality. As a daily exercise, try giving up all your worldly (evil) desires. This can mean not cursing, not gossiping, not catching an attitude, forgiving others, and so on. Read Galatians chapter five. You will find a list of the deeds of the flesh. Avoid them at all costs.

Sacrificing your will to do the will of God is difficult because you are used to being in charge as your own lord and master. Now, you will have to make Jesus Lord of your life and absolutely surrender to him.

It will also mean that you should employ the fruit of God's Spirit and apply it in all that you do. Again, Galatians chapter 5 will list them. It all happens in prayer where we submit to the revealed will of God and seek earnestly to apply it in our daily actions. The buzz words for step #1 are **Apply! Apply! Apply!**

When you example the deeds of the flesh, you conform to this world. When you apply or walk in the fruit of God's Holy Spirit, you confirm your Christianity, and establish your life's path and destiny.

So, to accomplish step #1, we must identify all that is of this world that offends God and deny it access into our thoughts and lifestyle. Here is what I do…I go to my Heavenly Father in prayer and offer myself to him as an instrument of his good pleasure. I join with my wife in daily prayer, pleading the "Blood of Christ" over all that we have and are. I give everything I own or will ever have to God, for his glory and I bind Satan and every other evil force away from my dwelling, family, and possessions. I do this in the name of Jesus.

Now here comes the hard part. During the day, as evil forces suggest lustful actions, I fight with all I have, in the name of Jesus, to cast them down and away from me. Then I draw near to God and cry out for help to overcome the inward desires of the flesh and/or the outward temptations that seek to torment me.

Sometimes I win. Sometimes I don't. However, when I fail, I know that I have an advocate with my Heavenly Father. That advocate is none other than Jesus, my Lord and Savor. (I John 2:1) He speaks for me before the throne of God and his blood cleanses me from all unrighteousness. (I John 1:9) So I go on sacrificing my inward life of sin, denying it at every turn and receiving the Holy Spirit of promise. I thus become a, "Living Sacrifice". It is working for me and it can also work for you.

Step #1

Step one is the beginning of knowing what is true and what is not. It is the foundation for shaping a reality that is pleasing to God.

Author's Note: About now, you are probably saying, "This is too much for me. I did not sign up for this sort of stuff." Well, what did you sign up for? Was it fire insurance to keep you out of hell? Was it to get stuff from God? If you are not willing to apply scripture to your life situations, you will remain alone as the seed that Jesus spoke of. Read all about it here:

According to the Bible, **Luke 1:24**, Jesus said that "unless a kernel of wheat falls to the ground and dies, it remains only a single seed, but if it dies, "it produces many seeds" (John 12:24). NKJ

Jesus also said…" If any man come to me, and hate not his father, and mother, and wife, and children, and brethren, and sisters, yea, and his own life also, he cannot be my disciple. And whosoever doth not bear his cross, and come after me, cannot be my disciple." NKJ

The point is, Jesus must be first and foremost in your life. He must be Lord of all or he is not Lord at all. It is like giving up the better to get the best. Sacrifice is painful, but the rewards are great.

Step #2

Change Your Thought Life

After you have mastered being a, "Living Sacrifice", at least trying every day, the next step is to **Change Your Thought Life…**Proverbs 23:7 said, "**For as he thinketh in his heart, so is he:**" We are what we think.

Have you ever evaluated the thoughts that flow through your mind? I have and I cannot keep up with them. They come at me so fast and are like fleeting images that zips away in a flash, leaving me blessed or cursed as they go.

What we allow to enter our minds is the raw material that is used to shape the reality we experience. Think about it. A man that watches pornographic videos, fills his mind with lustful acts against women. His thought life becomes pornographic and his actions vile and corrupt.

On the other hand, a man that reads the Bible and receives divine revelation from God fills his mind with truth and is set free from the snares of the devil and the habitual practice of sin. Do this and you will see your reality change and your spirit shifting from darkness unto light.

The apostle John tells us that we will know the truth and it will set us free. The freedom Jesus offers is a *spiritual* freedom from the bondage of a sinful lifestyle. **John 8:32**

Jesus is the Truth (John 14:6). Knowing the Truth will bring liberty. You will be free from sin, free from condemnation, and free from death. (Romans 6:22; 8:1–2)

So then…to be transformed by the renewing of our minds, we need to control the thoughts that enter our minds. Can we really do this in a world where almost every TV ad has a sexual overtone and movies portray violence? Yes, we can do it, but it will require some effort on our part. Listen to Paul again as he writes to the Corinthians:

"For though we walk in the flesh, we do not war after the flesh: (For the weapons of our warfare are not carnal, (earthly), but mighty through God to the pulling down of strongholds;) casting down imaginations, and every high thing that exalts itself against the knowledge of God, and bringing into captivity every thought to the obedience of Christ; And having in a readiness to revenge all disobedience, when your obedience is fulfilled." II Corinthians 10:4-6

Here Are Four Key Points To Consider:

- We must be in obedience to the revealed will of God. That is to say, *"Live Up To The Light You Have Been Given"*
- We must capture every thought that is against what God has revealed to you. If it goes against the Word of God, bring it into captivity using the knowledge of God. (*What you know to be true*)
- We are to cast every wrong thought down (*Give it no place in your thought life*.)
- We are to take upon ourselves a tone or attitude of revenge against thoughts that suggest disobedience or lawlessness. (*Fight back with all your might.*)

I remember a time when I drifted away from God. It was a terrible time of sadness and confusion. When I finally heard from my Lord, it was in the Spirit. He said, "John? It's a long way back. Are you willing to take the journey?" I immediately said, yes Lord. Then I heard him say again, "Your heart is like a field that now is full of thorns and weeds. We will have to pull up all the bad stuff and replant good seed. However, I will not leave you alone. We will do it together." Jesus and I have been cleaning up my heart ever since and planting the Word of God. As a result of all the effort, my thought life is better and my reality is different. It is better than it was before.

Sources of Thoughts

Believe it or not, all thoughts you think are not your own. I have noticed the following sources of thoughts:

- **The Devil**…he sends," Fiery Darts" that are meant to pierce our souls and destroy our dreams.
- **God**…who sends us divine revelation, unction and truths

- **People**…Their voices are constantly in our heads as they try to dominate us, sway our judgments, and put us under their pecking order.
- **The, "Old Man"** …We can and do think independently of others. However, the, "Old Man", otherwise known as "The Flesh" is constantly spreading negative thoughts in front of us. His voice is loud and always says, "I can handle it by myself."

So…what are you thinking about? Examine your thoughts; toss out what is wrong or offensive to God and hang on to what God says is good. Hold everything in the light of the knowledge of God (The Bible) and stand in the belief that you are God's child and therefore victorious over sin, death, Satan, hell, bad people, depressing circumstances or whatever.

I look for the source of the thought and then act accordingly. Sometimes the thought will overwhelm you and even torment you before you can figure it out. That's ok because the battle is not over until you fight back and cast it down. The way to win is to make a declaration of faith.

Jesus used the scriptures as his declaration of faith when confronted by evil. He said things like,

- Matthew 4:4, "**Man shall not live by bread alone, but by every word that proceeds out of the mouth of God**".
- And Luke 4:12, "And Jesus answering said unto him, It is said, **"Thou shalt not tempt the Lord thy God"**
- **"Get thee behind me Satan" Matthew 16:23.**

Step #2 (Day Two) is an exercise in applying the Word of God to destroy bad thoughts, no matter where they come from. This is your path to a new reality that will be pleasing to God.

You can measure your day-to-day progress by examining your thoughts. After a while, that which you battle will no longer show up at your door.

The secret is to apply what Paul told the 1st century church. He said, "Finally, brethren, whatsoever things are true, whatsoever things are honest, whatsoever things are just, whatsoever things are pure, whatsoever things are lovely, whatsoever things are of good report; if there be any virtue, and if there be any praise, ***think on these things***." Philippians 4:8

Step #3

Stay In A Continual Attitude of Prayer

We are admonished to, "Pray Without Ceasing**.**" 1 Thessalonians 5:17 No one can pray continually, but we can strive to stay in an attitude of conversational prayer, talking to God about our day, our dreams, and our destiny. We can even cast our cares upon him because he cares for us and wants to help us overcome. (I Peter 5:7)

Holy Spirit Interaction

This 3rd step in renewing our minds is to establish a relationship with the Holy Spirit and listen to what he has to say. His participation and your submission are vital to the success of your renewal.

Some of my unsaved friends laugh when I tell them I talk to God. They jokingly say, "Does he talk back to you?" I told them, "Yes, he sure does." God has spoken to us through the Bible. He left us over 3,000 promises to dwell on and 66 books written over thousands of years to read and meditate in.

I can surely say that I know God. I saw him first in the scriptures. He is there in full array. You can see his character; feel his compassion; discover his will for your life; and be taught by him personally.

If you question the idea of talking to the Holy Spirit, read what he is doing in your life even now. Instead of denying his presence, reach out to him and strengthen your bond of love with God. Here are a few scriptures to ponder: Listen to what the Bible says about the Holy Spirit's interaction with the child of God.

1. "And I will pray the Father, and he shall give you another Comforter, that he may abide with you forever;" John 14:16

2. "The Spirit itself bears witness with our spirit, that we are the children of God:" Romans 8:15

3. "The Helper, the Holy Spirit, whom the Father will send in my name, will teach you everything and make you remember all that I have told you." (John 14:26)

4. "When they finished praying, the place where they were meeting was shaken. They were all filled with the Holy Spirit and began to proclaim God's message with boldness." (Acts 4:31)

5. "In the same way the Spirit also comes to help us, weak as we are. For we do not know how we ought to pray; the Spirit himself pleads with God for us in groans that words cannot express." (Romans 8:26)

6. "When you heard the message of truth, the gospel of your salvation, and when you believed in him, you were also sealed with the promised Holy Spirit. He is the down payment of our inheritance, for the redemption of the possession, to the praise of his glory." Ephesians 1:13-14

7. "Now there are varieties of gifts, but the same Spirit, and there are varieties of ministries, but the same Lord. There are varieties of results, but it is the same God who produces all the results in everyone. To each person has been given the ability to manifest the Spirit for the common good." I Corinthians 12:1-11.

8. "For all who are led by God's Spirit are God's children." Romans 8:14.

9. "What? know ye not that your body is the temple of the Holy Ghost which is in you, which ye have of God, and ye are not your own?" 1 Corinthians 6:19.

10. "For his Spirit searches out everything and shows us God's deep secrets. No one can know a person's thoughts except that person's own spirit, and no one can know God's thoughts except God's own Spirit. And we have received God's Spirit (not the world's spirit), so we can know the wonderful things God has freely given us. When we tell you these things, we do not use words that come from human wisdom. Instead, we speak words given to us by the Spirit, using the Spirit's words to explain spiritual truths." 1 Corinthians 2:7-13.

11. "for the kingdom of God is not eating and drinking, but righteousness, peace, and joy in the Holy Spirit." Romans 14:17

12. "And be not drunk with wine, wherein is excess; but be filled with the Spirit;" Ephesians 5:18

Do not be afraid to talk to the Holy Spirit. He is given to us as a Teacher, Guide, Comforter, Seal of Redemption, and he brings gifts that edify us and bless the body of our Lord, the church.

Stay tuned in and you will hear from God and discover his will for your life. This is the third step in renewing your mind. I call it *"Practicing the Presence of God."* Remember, it's just conversational prayer in which you give God the authority to operate in your life, counsel you and guide you.

Step #4

Always Be Thankful

There is too much negativity in this world. It seems as though life is mostly sad and depressing. I guess that's because of a liberal media that is bent on showing all the bad stuff. You would think that there is nothing happening that is good. Well, God wants us to see only the good. He wants us to be happy, have life in abundance, and to always be thankful. Listen to what the Word of God says on this subject.

"In everything give thanks: for this is the will of God in Christ Jesus concerning you." 1 Thessalonians 5:18

I know that you are questioning this step. How can we give thanks in everything. When things get bad and we suffer, how can we be thankful?

Most folks blame God for bad things that come their way. We should remember that God is a God of Love and has not dealt with us after our own sin. (Psalm 103:10) We are not being punished. You've heard it said that "It rains on the just and the unjust", right?

Hear Peter in I Peter 5:8 "Be sober, be vigilant; because your adversary the devil, as a roaring lion, walks about, seeking whom he may devour."

The devil is hard at work trying to devour us but in verse nine Peter tells us what to do…" Whom resist steadfast in the faith, knowing that the same afflictions are accomplished in your brethren that are in the world."

You should know we are not to give thanks for the thing that is attacking us. (In everything, not for everything) That means we are to look for the good and focus our energies on the blessings of our Lord in that situation. Here is an example:

You get into a car accident. It was not your fault. You are not hurt, just shaken up a bit, even though the car is totaled. You have two choices.

1.) to concentrate on the loss of your car and the stupidity of the other driver and tell everyone you know about your loss. This will gather sympathy and some will even console you.

2.) To concentrate on the fact that God kept you safe from harm and you didn't get hurt. This will glorify God in the situation and draw you closer to him as you see his hand in your life.

Now, I also know that sometimes things are hard to deal with and cause much grief like the loss of a loved one, a loss of a good-paying job, kids going astray, divorce, etc. Even these hard things to bear have a glimmer of light and hope for the future. Listen again to the scriptures as Paul writes in Romans 8:28-31.

"And we know, that all things work together for good to them that love

God, to them who are the called according to his purpose. For whom he did foreknow, he also did predestinate to be conformed to the image of his Son, that he might be the firstborn among many brethren. Moreover, whom he did predestinate, them he also called: and whom he called, them he also justified: and whom he justified, them he also glorified. What shall we then say to these things? If God be for us, who can be against us?" Romans 8:28-31

We can still hang on to the fact that we are called according to his purposes. We love God and therefore are assured that all things will work together for our good.

Being thankful and giving thanks to God is a, "MINDSET". We resolve to not blame God; to always see the good and never dwell on the negative. It's hard to get depressed, become angry or dwell in negativity when you are thanking God for every little and big thing. In every situation, we bless God and trust him to work on our behalf.

Step #5

Believe That Every Day Is A New Day

Have you ever encountered a person who lives in the past? They are all around us. They seem to live in the past or in the future but seldom in today. They plan for the future, cry over the past and hide from reality because today is too close and has too many unexpected events that force them to deal now in a confrontational posture.

Hear what the Bible says about TODAY…" ***This is the day which the LORD hath made; we will rejoice and be glad in it." Psalm 118:24***

If we believe that every day is the day that the Lord has made, it will be easier to live out that day, knowing he has created it just for us. We can indeed, rejoice and be glad in it.

Hear what the Bible says about God's mercy in every new day… "***God's mercies are new every morning" (Lamentations 3:23).***

We also know, without a doubt, that God's mercy, (Unmerited Favor), is new every morning. That means he does not hate us for what went on yesterday. He may be disappointed but we are his children and thus subject to his correction. He leads us to repentance and starts all over again, as if yesterday never happened.

We need to avoid the, **"If Only"** trap. You know what I mean? "If only I did better in my marriage" "If only I said no to drugs" "If only" … you added the thing that you most hate and wish it had never happened. These things can become strongholds that capture our thoughts and keep us in bondage.

I feel good about "TODAY" because God made it for me. Therefore, I can let tomorrow take care of itself and drop yesterday from my thinking. God is not mad at me. His Holy Spirit is with me and will help my infirmities. Romans 8:26)

The above statement reflects the attitude that will transform you as you use it to renew your mind. However, you should know another thing that Paul says about this renewal.

In Ephesians 4:23 Paul used a striking phrase to parallel Romans 12:2. He said, **"Be renewed in the spirit of your minds."** Now what in the world is that? "The spirit of your mind." It means that the mind has a "spirit." In other words, our mind has what we call a *"mindset."* It doesn't just have a view. It has a viewpoint. It doesn't just have the power to perceive and detect; it also has a posture, a demeanor, a bearing, an attitude, a bent. "Be renewed in the **spirit** of your mind."

Day Five and all days are steps in the renewal process that form a "Mindset" in which we move, live, and have our existence. The belief that," Every Day Is A New Day", is part of that mindset. Live in that perspective and you will find God's will and live out his destiny for your life.

God wants us to have his mind (his thoughts, his viewpoint) in every situation. He wants us to have the supernatural ability to discern everything that happens from his vantage point and his perspective. If we can see from his perspective, we will be able to "soar" above our circumstances, leaving our problems and trials behind.

Step #6

Guard Your Spirit

In Step #2, I discussed changing your thought life. Now I would like to further develop that, so you have a deeper understanding.

Proverbs 23:7 said, "**For as he thinks in his heart, so is he:**" We are what we think. Jesus talked about a man that committed adultery because he thought about having a sexual relationship with a woman that was not his wife.

"But I say unto you, that whosoever looks upon a woman to lust after her hath committed adultery with her already in his heart." (Matthew 5:28) We do not want to fall into this trap.

We need to guard our hearts so those types of feelings do not overwhelm us. They are rooted in lust and will defile us.

It's important to understand that the devil will shoot "Fiery Darts" at us that draw us away from God into our own lustful nature. Sometimes we cannot stop the attack, but we can reject its suggestive allure. In other words, we do not have to participate.

Listen to the scriptures…" Watch over your heart with all diligence, for from it flows the springs of life**. Put away from you a deceitful mouth, and put devious speech far from you. Let your eyes look directly ahead and let your gaze be fixed straight in front of you. Watch the path of your feet, and all your ways will be established." – Proverbs 4:23-26 (emphasis added)

Thoughts Cause Feelings and Affect Emotions

We all know that some people are more emotional than others. Some even wear their emotions on their shoulder…they are very sensitive. Others are like a rock, seemingly unaffected by life's many trials. Regardless of how we feel, we are all subject to a continual flow of thoughts and we must guard our hearts. It is there that we ponder and evaluate and make decisions that are expressed by our emotions.

What comes out of our hearts is what defiles us:

And he said, "What comes out of a person is what defiles him. For from within, out of the heart of man, come evil thoughts, sexual immorality, theft, murder, adultery, coveting, wickedness, deceit, sensuality, envy, slander, pride, foolishness. All these evil things come from within, and they defile a person."–Mark 7:20-23

If we want to know what is in our hearts, we need only to listen to what is flowing out of our mouths. Curse words, hate, anger, fear and the like are of the flesh. However, they flow out because they are already inside. They come from a fallen nature. We also add to that evil when we accept new destructive thoughts. They are added to what is already there.

On the other hand, if we are filled with God's Spirit, we will experience the fruit of the Spirit and our mouths will flow with expressions of Love, Peace, Joy, Longsuffering, Kindness, and the other fruit listed in Galatians chapter five.

We are the channels through which good and evil flow. That is why we are admonished to "GUARD" our hearts…because the issues of life come forth from what is inside. We can allow evil or good to manifest. This forms the basis of our day.

So…our day-to-day reality depends upon what we think and what we allow to be planted in our hearts. My wife has a saying that I like and often repeat. She said, *"Let's not go down that road"*. We often use this phrase when our nerves are frayed and we are on the verge of an argument. I also use it when I think things I shouldn't think. I said, "I am not going there" "Get behind me Satan." Then I call upon the Lord to deliver me from that temptation. I don't always do the right thing here, but I try my best to apply this truth. I am trying and so can you, even if we fail now and then. We can still get up and try again.

Step # 7

Listen For The Whistle

If you watch football, you will relate to this. You are watching the game and see a player go off sides. The camera focused on the off-side act and then the referee, who immediately blows a loud whistle, points straight at the player and screams out, "Off Sides". That's an excellent picture of what Paul is saying to the Galatians' church. Take a listen…

"And let the peace of God rule in your hearts, to the which also ye are called in one body; and be ye thankful." Colossians 3:15

There will be times when confusion will cloud your thought life and you will not see clearly. It will be hard to know what to do. Using the "Peace of God" as a referee will fix all of that.

If you do not have peace from God about the thoughts that trouble you, toss them out. If you feel only confusion in a situation, do not act. Wait until you have peace before acting. When making decisions, seek God for counsel and ensure that you are in a state of "PEACE". Always allow the "Peace of God" to be the referee. The God of peace will blow a whistle if you are off sides and tell you to get back where you belong.

Peace is a state of tranquility or quietness of spirit that transcends circumstances. The term *peace* is described in Scripture as a gift of the Holy Spirit and reflects his character (1 Thessalonians 5:23; Galatians 6:16; 1 Peter 1:2; Hebrews 13:20).

If we are filled with his Spirit, we will have access to and experience the peace of God. We can rest assured that God will use his peace, as Colossians 3:15 suggests. However, Paul does not say that all this happens without our agreement. God will not violate our free will. That's why Paul said, "Let" or "allow" because to "let" is to be under submission and in concert with. It takes a simple prayer each day to be filled with the Spirit and in agreement that God's peace will be our "Whistle Blower." Thus, we give the Holy spirit the authority to referee our lives and alert us when we are off sides.

Jesus said, "Peace I leave with you; my peace I give to you. Not as the world gives do I give to you. Let not your hearts be troubled, neither let them be afraid" (John 14:27).

It's ok to let the Holy Spirit be your referee. He will not lead you astray. His job is to bring you into the image of Christ and show you the way to glory so you can walk with dignity and glorify God here on this earth.

Certain attitudes can destroy the peace of God. When we equate trust with the assumption that God will give us whatever we want, we set ourselves up for disappointment. The Bible is filled with examples of the opposite happening to

God's people (2 Corinthians 12:7–9; Hebrews 11:13; Psalm 10:1).

Trust means we have set our hearts to believe God, whatever may happen. When we insist on being in control, we sabotage God's desire to let us live in peace. When we choose worry rather than faith, we cannot live in peace. Jesus warned us often about fear and worry (Matthew 6:34; Luke 12:29; Philippians 4:6). Worry is the enemy of peace. God invites us to cast our cares upon him and then let go of them (1 Peter 5:7). If we listen, we will hear that whistle blowing and the voice of God telling us to trust in him.

Psalm 91:1 holds the secret to living in the "Peace of God:" "He that dwells in the secret place of the "Most High" shall abide under the shadow of the Almighty. I will say of the LORD, He is my refuge and my fortress: my God; in him will I trust."

That secret place is in the presence of God, where we can live in his Spirit. That is where we meet God and have fellowship. When we walk in his

Spirit, we experience all that God is and adorn his very character. We actually fulfill his desire to create man is his image and likeness. (Gen.1:26) It is here, under the shadow of his wings, that we can remain peaceful, even when circumstances are not. When we learn to cry out to him in times of trouble, we find that his peace really passes all human understanding (Philippians 4:7).

Allowing the "Peace of God" to be your referee in all decision making. His peace will keep you on the right track as you renew your mind. It is part of the process to attain and enjoy the reality of God.

CHAPTER TWO:
"HOW TO" MOVE ON BEYOND TRANSFORMATION

Once you have become accustomed to practicing the seven steps, you will want to move on. However, "Moving On" is spiritual, not carnal, or earthly. I found that I needed to walk in the Spirit, not the flesh. It was hard at first, but as I struggled and made a conscious effort, it became easier. We will talk more about this in chapter three.

As I applied the seven-step method to my everyday life, I began to see key factors that helped me along the way. They were like runway lights that lit up the path so I could land safely.

Moving on means just that. God will not drag you down the road of life. He will, however, show you the way. Sometimes, he must create a way where there is no way. In the final analysis, it is our "Free Will" choices that move us on towards our divine destiny. (We look for a reality that is pleasing to God.)

If I am sad and unhappy, I will need to shift my thinking to those things that make me happy. This will put me in another reality that is more livable. I call this "Reality Squared". It does not dissolve the sad reality. It is still there, looming over my soul. But…I am no longer there. I have moved on emotionally by thinking about new or better things.

It is not an easy thing to do, but it is possible. It requires rejection of the sad and acceptance of the happy. Try singing a cheerful song or recalling a pleasurable experience. Laugh, just for the fun of it. The trick is to do something positive, even when you don't want to.

I often said to a friend that she should "Break A Face" when she was depressed. Do it no matter how you feel. If you can laugh at the world and things that irritate you, you will retain a healthy mental attitude which will sustain your walk into the future.

I believe that we "Move On" from one reality to another. When I was a child, I thought and acted like a child. But now that I am an adult, I have put away childish things and become a responsible individual. Read it from the Bible:

"When I was a child, I spoke as a child, I felt as a child, I thought as a child: now that I am become a man, I have put away childish things." I Corinthians 13:11 ASV

As an adult, we see life differently and believe based upon perspectives that were never considered when we were a child. As we mature into adults, we often drawn new beliefs that change how we think and act in this world. These beliefs can create a new lifestyle that can be pleasing to God or even be a reality that leaves out God depending on our free will choices.

Note: Passing through multiple realities in life is common to all experiences. However, this sliding through dimensional reality is only a part of true reality. Remember, true reality is ***the total of everything that exists.*** That includes all that is actually in existence which goes beyond our individuality.

However, that said, individual reality is what we are focusing on right now and that is defined as a point of view or perspective that governs our daily lives and rules our thought-life. That is why the apostle Paul pleaded with the church to be transformed…in other words, your current thought patterns are leading you down a road that leads to destruction. Renewing your mind will bring you back to the right path in life that takes you into the glory of God and his divine will. This is the "Reality of God"

Paul did not care about everything that existed in his day. He cared about the lives of those that were under his care. He wanted them to be loyal disciples and fulfill their God-given destiny.

It is important to be aware of all that exists in our world, but we do not have to accept everything it offers. Example: It may be actual and real that some folks do evil things as a lifestyle. But we can choose not to take part in what they are doing. Their individual reality is leading them to hell whereas, our individual reality is headed towards an eternity with God.

Renewal is at the heart of moving on. You cannot move on until you have been renewed. Let's look at some Bible verses that support this "Moving On" perspective:

John 3:3 &3:16…." Verily, verily, I say unto thee, except a man be born again, he cannot see the kingdom of God."" For God so loved the world, that he gave his only begotten Son, that whosoever believeth in him should not perish, but have everlasting life."

Moving on requires a, "New Birth" that would qualify us to see the kingdom of God. Jesus was speaking to Nicodemus, a religious leader of his day. In other words, Jesus said that religion does not offer eternal life. The only way to attain that was to believe on him as the only begotten Son of God who was given to the world that it could be saved. This is another "Reality Squared" that must happen. We must receive Christ and that alone will move us on.

Philippians 3:13-16 …"Brethren, I count not myself to have apprehended: this one thing I do, forgetting those things which are behind and reaching forth unto those things which are before, I press toward the mark for the prize of the high calling of God in Christ Jesus. Let us therefore, as many as be perfect,(Mature) be thus minded: and if in anything ye be otherwise minded, God shall reveal even this unto you. Nevertheless, whereto we have already attained, let us walk by the same rule, let us mind the same thing."

Paul is looking at a new reality which he calls, *"The higher calling of God"* He also said to the church that to attain it, they must, like he is doing, leave the past and let it go so it has no more influence in our decision making. He cannot glory in past accomplishments or boast in his education or personal social status. His eyes are on what is ahead, in the future. A relationship with Jesus is the prize to attain. It is the reason for all the effort. It was his "Reality Squared."

Philippians 2:5-8…"Let this mind be in you, which was also in Christ Jesus: Who, being in the form of God, thought it not robbery to be equal with God: But made himself of no reputation, and took upon him the form of a servant, and was made in the likeness of men: And being found in fashion as a man, he humbled himself, and became obedient unto death, even the death of the cross."

Moving on is to allow the mind of Christ to dwell in you. That happens when we are filled with his Spirit. God does not force this upon us. He offers it as a "Free Will" choice. It is important to see the mind of Christ in its true form. Here's what I see:

- He humbled himself and gave up any self-recognition he might have to boast about…like being God.
- He became obedient to the will of God, the Father, sacrificing his own desires and ambition.
- He was willing to die for what he believed.
- He dedicated himself to his calling and remained steadfast in his thinking.
- Though he was king of all, he took upon himself the posture of a servant.

Galatians 2:20…" I am crucified with Christ: nevertheless, I live; yet not I, but Christ lives in me: and the life which I now live in the flesh I live by the faith of the Son of God, who loved me and gave himself for me."

Moving on is to be crucified with Christ…that is to say, consider yourself to be dead to the old sinful appetites and seek to walk in a new and living way. It means to depend on the faith of Jesus to sustain you and keep you. It means a total surrender to the life of Christ dwelling in you. That can only happen through Bible study and prayer. This is an attitude or posture that you must accept and live out in this world. It is another example of "Reality Squared."

Matthew 6:33… "But seek ye first the kingdom of God, and his righteousness; and all these things shall be added unto you."

Moving on is to seek first the kingdom of God and his righteousness. This relieves us of striving to be accepted in this world. We no longer have to live up to the expectations of others or fight to be somebody or attain wealth or stature. All that the world is seeking after will be added to us when we put God first. Life becomes less stressful when we depend upon the Lord. He knows our need and will provide when the time is right.

I Peter 5:7… "Casting all your care upon him; for he cares for you."

Moving on is made easy when we cast *all*, not some, but *all,* our cares upon the Lord, knowing that he really loves us and has our best interest at heart. If we could practice this truth, we would reduce our worry to zero. It is hard to worry over anything when you have given it to God. That is, unless you take it back. If Jesus is Lord, he will carry your load, fight your battles, and deliver you…or he will help you to get through the trials of life as the victor, not the victim.

Casting is like tossing it far away from us. We strive to not think about it and if we do, we immediately tell ourselves, "It's in the hands of Jesus. He will deal with it as he sees fit."

Proverbs 3:5-6…" Trust in the Lord with all thine heart; and lean not unto thine own understanding. In all thy ways acknowledge him, and he shall direct thy paths."

Moving on involves acknowledging the Lord and trusting in him to guide you into the future. He knows what is ahead and can lead you away from serious harm. Acknowledging him is to include him in every decision. There was an old saying that was popular when I was a young Christian. It goes like this, **"What would Jesus do?"** What would he do in this situation? His direction is based upon our acknowledgement of his authority, power, and love. It all boils down to seeking his will in all that we do. This is "Reality Squared," a posture to dawn or attain.

Hebrews 4:9-11…" There remains therefore a rest to the people of God. For he that is entered into his rest, he also hath ceased from his own works, as God did from his. Let us labor therefore to enter into that rest, lest any man fall after the same example of unbelief."

Moving on is to capture the vision of God's grace and how it works in the lives of his children. The text of Hebrews talks about the Old Testament saints that did not rest in the grace of God. Instead, they trusted in their own works of righteousness to save them. The writer of Hebrews is saying that we should not fall into their reality of salvation by works or man's effort. He continues to explain that we must reject any notion that we could ever be saved outside of God's unmerited favor. He further tells them to labor to enter in if necessary.

This is a big controversy in today's Christian thinking. Many denominations hold fast to salvation by works. They have fallen into the same lie that the foolish Galatians believed. But the writer of Hebrews tells us we are to rest in the finished work of Christ.

Jesus, himself said, as recorded in John 3:16 that "Whosoever" believes in him, would not perish but have eternal life. He has always been the way to God the Father. John 6:44 The children of God are the "Whosoever" folks that believed in Jesus.

Listen to what Paul tells the Galatian believers in the 1st century. "O foolish Galatians, who hath bewitched you, that ye should not obey the truth, before whose eyes Jesus Christ hath been evidently set forth, crucified among you? This only would I learn of you, Received ye the Spirit by the works of the law, or by the hearing of faith?" "Are ye so foolish? having begun in the Spirit, are ye now made perfect by the flesh? Have ye suffered so many things in vain? if it be yet in vain. He therefore that ministered to you the Spirit, and worketh miracles among you, doeth he it by the works of the law, or by the hearing of faith?

Even as Abraham believed God, and it was accounted to him for righteousness.

Know ye therefore that they which are of faith, the same are the children of Abraham. And the scripture, foreseeing that God would justify the heathen through faith, preached before the gospel unto Abraham saying, In thee shall all nations be blessed. So then they which be of faith are blessed with faithful Abraham. For as many as are of the works of the law are under the curse: for it is written, Cursed *is* every one that continues not in all things which are written in the book of the law to do them. But that no man is justified by the law in the sight of God, *it is* evident: for, The just shall live by faith.

And the law is not of faith: but, The man that doeth them shall live in them. Christ hath redeemed us from the curse of the law, being made a curse for us: for it is written, Cursed *is* every one that hangs on a tree: That the blessing of Abraham might come on the Gentiles through Jesus Christ; that we might receive the promise of the Spirit through faith.

Brethren, I speak after the manner of men; Though *it be* but a man's covenant, yet *if it be* confirmed, no man disannuls, or adds thereto. Now to Abraham and his seed were the promises made. He saith not, And to seeds, as of many; but as of one, And to thy seed, which is Christ. And this I say, *that* the covenant, that was confirmed before of God in Christ, the law, which was four hundred and thirty years after, cannot disannul, that it should make the promise of none effect.

For if the inheritance *be* of the law, *it is* no more of promise: but God gave *it* to Abraham by promise. Wherefore then *serves* the law? It was added because of transgressions, till the seed should come to whom the promise was made; *and it was* ordained by angels in the hand of a mediator.

Now a mediator is not *a mediator* of one, but God is one. Is the law then against the promises of God? God forbid: for if there had been a law given which could have given life, verily righteousness should have been by the law. But the scripture hath concluded all under sin, that the promise by faith of Jesus Christ might be given to them that believe.

But before faith came, we were kept under the law, shut up unto the faith which should afterwards be revealed. Wherefore, the law was our schoolmaster to bring us unto Christ, that we might be justified by faith.

But after that faith is come, we are no longer under a schoolmaster. For ye are all the children of God by faith in Christ Jesus. For as many of you as have been baptized into Christ have put on Christ. There is neither Jew nor Greek, there is neither bond nor free, there is neither male nor female: for ye are all one in Christ Jesus. And if ye be Christ's, then are ye Abraham's seed, and heirs according to the promise." Galatians 3:1-29.

I added the entire chapter to my text so you could see the truth for yourself. We are saved by grace through faith. It is a gift of God, lest anyone should boast. Ephesians 2:8-9.

Moving on is to rest in God, knowing that Jesus paid the price of our redemption. This is another "Reality Squared" that we must attain. Without it, we will be most miserable.

Romans 4:17… (as it is written, "I have made you a father of many nations") in the presence of him whom he believed—God, who gives life to the dead and calls those things which do not exist as though they did"

Moving on is agreeing with God, even when you do not see it. Romans 4:17 says that God spoke to Abraham and called him the father of many nations long before it actually happened. God can see far into our future and often calls something forth that does not exist, giving it life. He will do that with all his children. He will speak over you, calling forth his divine destiny.

We are to believe that what he said will indeed come true and also speak it forth, calling it into existence. That is what Abraham did and God honored him, saying it was accounted unto him for righteousness. His belief by faith established his righteousness, not his works. That's why he is called the faithful. Now, let's not get off track. We can call things forth into existence like faithful Abraham, but there are conditions.

We cannot call forth a new car or a mansion or a new house and think it will suddenly appear. What we can call forth is what God has spoken into our lives. That's what Abraham did, and that's what we can do.

The question at hand is…what has God spoken into your life? Whatever it is, call it forth by faith and believe that it will suddenly appear for he makes ways where there are no ways and paths where there are no paths. He will move mountains if need be.

Romans 8:28-30…" And we know that all things work together for good to them that love God, to them who are the called according to his purpose. For whom he did foreknow, he also did predestinate to be conformed to the image of his Son, that he might be the firstborn among many brethren. Moreover, whom he did predestinate, them he also called: and whom he called, them he also justified: and whom he justified, them he also glorified."

Moving on is to know, without a shadow of a doubt, that all things will work together for your good. However, this promise is for only those who are called according to his purposes and fear (Reverence) God. This is another "Reality Squared," a picture of the hand of God working in the lives of his children to bless them, no matter what.

Note the predestination. He predetermines their destination. It was to be Christ-like. The reason for such an act of grace is to honor Jesus as the firstborn among many brethren. Those that have been chosen by the John 3:16 doctrine were justified and glorified. However, not by their own efforts, but by Christ and his finished work of grace on the cross.

I am sure you will see many more "Moving On" scriptures. Value them and apply them in your life. I see them as different realities that we go through as we walk with Jesus. Some would say it is growing in your faith. Others would call it moving from glory to glory. In any event, it is, in my humble opinion, "Reality Squared," a process of redemption and a path to being free in Christ. It is a quest to discover Biblical truth and false teaching.

Chapter Three: "How To" Walk in the Spirit of God

Remember, we are moving from the flesh into the Spirit, from darkness into God's light, and from death unto life. We must learn how to walk in the Spirit to please God and attain his reality.

Ephesians 5:18 "And be not drunk with wine, wherein is excess; but be filled

with the Spirit."

What are the benefits? Only this:

- He will confirm to us that we are really God's children.
- He will baptize us in his Spirit, enhancing our life and personality.
- He will counsel us as to what to do in any situation.
- He will guide us to a place of safety and freedom.
- He will break every yoke of bondage that now holds us captive.
- He will give us peace that passes all understanding.
- There are more, but this will suffice for now.

Being filled with the Spirit is a conscious choice. It does not just happen.

If it did, Paul would not have said for us to be filled. I realize that we receive the Holy Spirit at our "New Birth" and automatically become his temple. However, demonstrating his character every day requires a submission to him and a fresh infilling or anointing. This is needed because our flesh wars against God's Spirit for control of our minds. The winner gets to reveal the good or evil therein…so we must yield ourselves to the Spirit and receive him daily.

It seems that we are always in a struggle between good and evil. They fight for our approval and life applications. The world influences us with power, fame, pride, and riches. It says that we can have it all and be like God, a god unto ourselves. This is far from the truth.

The only way to escape its influence is to walk in the Spirit, not the flesh. Here is what the Bible says, "This I say then, walk in the Spirit, and ye shall not fulfil the lust of the flesh." Galatians 5:16

The Spirit is the Holy Spirit. He is the ultimate reality. We are faced with two distinct realities, flesh, and Spirit. Our "free will" choices will determine our lifestyle, destiny, path in life, and happiness. Let's look at the fruit of God's Spirit and the deeds of the flesh. They are found in Galatians, chapter five.

" Now **the works of the flesh** are manifest, which are *these*; Adultery, fornication, uncleanness, lasciviousness, idolatry, witchcraft, hatred, variance, emulations, wrath, strife, seditions, heresies, envying, murders, drunkenness, revellings, and such like: of the which, I tell you before, as I have also told you in time past, that they which do such things shall not inherit the kingdom of God.

But **the fruit of the Spirit** is love, joy, peace, longsuffering, gentleness, goodness, faith, meekness, temperance: against such there is no law. And they that are Christ's have crucified the flesh with the affections and lusts. If we live in the Spirit, let us also walk in the Spirit." Galatians 5:18-25

We also learn in Galatians that, "the flesh lusts against the Spirit and the

Spirit against the flesh: and they are contrary the one to the other: so that you cannot do the things you would" Galatians 5:17

I will explain each gift and fruit with definitions to be sure accuracy and clarity are maintained.

Our study will look at the operation of gifts and fruits in the believer's life. I will address such questions as:

- Do all gifts apply?
- Are gifts more important than fruit?
- Which gift is the best gift?
- How do I know what fruit I have and which gifts are in operation?
- Are there other gifts not mentioned in the Bible that I could obtain?
- And other questions of interest.

My desire is to inform, educate, counsel, and be a blessing to new and growing Christians so they can develop a deeper understanding of the Holy Spirit and his operation in their lives.

This study does not aim to endorse one group over another. Most of us are aware of the "Charismatic Renewal" that swept through the church in the last 50 years. This renewal focused on the Holy Spirit and the use of "Gifts" in the believer's life. Many new denominations and independent groups have sprung up around the world. There is, however, an ongoing controversy between main line protestant and charismatic groups on the gifts of the Holy Spirit and if they are applicable for today.

The fruit of the Spirit is widely accepted by most all Christian groups. It is the single most evidence of being a real follower of Christ.

I will look into the fruit of the Spirit and the gifts of the Spirit to determine their validly, use in daily life and purposes for the church of today. Both are part of God's reality.

The Gifts of The Holy Spirit

When I was a young Christian, my church taught that the gifts passed away with the deaths of the apostles. They used a text in I Corinthians 13:8-10, "Charity never fails: but whether there be prophecies, they shall fail; whether there be tongues, they shall cease; whether there be knowledge, it shall vanish away. For we know in part, and we prophesy in part, but, when *that which is perfect* is come, then that which is in part shall be done away"

Paul has told the church that the time will come when the gifts will no longer be needed. The error in the reading by most mainline churches is the timing. Paul told us the timing will be when "*That which is perfect* has come."

"*That which is perfect* has come…" This can only be a reference to the coming of the perfect one, Jesus. (Paul said this after Jesus' resurrection, referring to his 2nd coming.) Until that time, the gifts are in effect and needed in the church to validate its existence.

Paul said, "For now we see through a glass, darkly; but then face to face: now I know in part; but then shall I know even as also I am known." I Corinthians 13:12 We have yet to see Jesus, the perfect one, face to face.

Listen to I Corinthians 13:1-7, "Though I speak with the tongues of men and of angels, and have not charity, (Love), I am become *as* sounding brass, or a tinkling cymbal. And though I have the gift of prophecy, and understand all mysteries, and all knowledge; and though I have all faith, so that I could remove mountains, and have not charity, I am nothing. And though I bestow all my goods to feed the poor, and though I give my body to be burned, and have not charity, it profits me nothing.

Charity (or Love) suffers long, and is kind; charity envies not; charity vaunts not itself, is not puffed up, does not behave itself unseemly, seeks not her own, is not easily provoked, thinks no evil; Rejoices not in iniquity, but rejoices in the truth; bears all things, believeth all things, hopes all things, endures all things."

The above scriptures are a masterful presentation of how fruit and gifts operate together in the life of a believer. The gifts operate through Love, which is a fruit. Otherwise, the administration of the gift is like a person singing off key.

Fruit of The Spirit

Let's look more closely at the fruit of the spirit before we get into the gifts. I was always taught that there is only one fruit. Even the Bible refers to the "Fruit" as in singular. Then, the fruit manifests itself into nine different functions. The Bible in Galatians 5:22 mentions love, joy, peace, long-suffering, gentleness, goodness, faith, meekness, and temperance as the fruit of the Spirit. Together, they reveal the character or personality of God.

When someone wants to know what God is like, they can point to these attributes to explain. Also, when you want to know what Love is, you can look no further than right here. Here to is where you look to analyze a person's love. Are they like this? If so, then you know they are of God and worthy of your love in return.

Let us look at each one individually.

Love…God is love. His character is one of pure love. There is no evil in him.

God is Love, and his love is very different from human love. God's love is unconditional, and it's not based on feelings or emotions. He does not love us because we are lovable or because we make him feel good; He loves us because he is love. He created us to have a loving relationship with him, and he sacrificed his own Son (who also willingly died for us) to restore that relationship.

"But God commended his love toward us, in that, while we were yet sinners, Christ died for us." Romans 5:8 In this verse and John 3:16, we find no conditions placed on God's love for us. God does not say, "As soon as you clean up your act, I'll love you;" nor does he say, "I'll sacrifice my Son if you promise to love me."

In fact, in Romans 5:8, we find just the opposite. God wants us to know that his love is unconditional, so he sent his Son, Jesus Christ, to die for us while we were still unlovable sinners. We didn't have to get clean, and we didn't have to make any promises to God before we could experience his love. His love for us has always existed, and because of that, he did all the giving and sacrificing long before we knew even that we needed his love.

Joy …Joy is a state of mind and an orientation of the heart. It is a settled state of contentment, confidence, and hope. It is something or someone that provides a source of happiness. It appears 88 times in the Old Testament in 22 books; 57 times in the New Testament in 18 books.

Christians should always find reasons to be joyful. There are many ways to define joy. Joy isn't just a smile or a laugh. Joy is something that is deep within and does not leave quickly. When we have the joy of the Lord, we will know it and so will others. Since joy is given by God and is something that he wants us to have, we need to be joyful! Besides being joyful, we should let others have their joy and not bring them down when they are excited about good things. **The only thing worse than not having joy is stealing someone else's.**

Ask for joy! If we cannot find reasons to be joyful, our perspective must have changed. God lets us have blessings every day. We should be able to see them and thank God for them. Additionally, we should ask for God's blessings! Some think they should be blessed with joy automatically, but God's Word said "You have not because you do not ask." (John 15:16)

God's Holy Spirit produces joy. Joy is a product of Christ-likeness. When we seek God through his Word and prayer, we will receive joy! Thank God that joy is something he wants us to have!

Joy is the second "fruit of the Spirit," according to Galatians 5:22, "But the fruit of the Spirit is…joy. "

Reading the scriptures will bring us joy! "And these things we write to you that your joy may be full." (1 John 1:4) We will also see where the Bible gives us specific times to be joyful.

Philippians 4:4 "Rejoice in the Lord always. Again, I will say, rejoice!"

Proverbs 12:20 "Deceit is in the heart of those who devise evil, but counselors of peace have joy."

Proverbs 21:15 "It is a joy for the just to do justice, but destruction will come to the workers of iniquity."

Nehemiah 8:10 "For the joy of the LORD is your strength."

Peace… The Hebrew Bible uses a familiar but significant word, "*shalom*". In its purest sense, *shalom* means "peace."

The connotation is positive. When someone says, "Shalom," or, "Peace unto you," it doesn't mean, "I hope you don't get into any trouble;" it means, "I hope you have all the highest good coming your way."

Most people in our world do not understand peace as a positive concept. All they know is the negative aspect of peace, which is merely the absence of trouble. The definition of peace in many languages of the world illustrates that. For example:

- the Quechua Indians in Ecuador and Bolivia use a word for peace that literally translates, "to sit down in one's heart." For them, peace is the opposite of running around in the midst of constant anxieties.
- the Chol Indians of Mexico define peace as "a quiet heart."

> Those may be beautiful ways to put it, but they still seem to leave us with only the negative idea that peace is the absence of trouble.

The Biblical concept of peace does not focus on the absence of trouble. Biblical peace is unrelated to circumstances; it is a goodness of life that is not touched by what happens on the outside. You may be in the midst of great trials and still have Biblical peace.

Paul said he could be content in any circumstance; and he demonstrated that he had peace even in the jail at Philippi, where he sang and remained confident that God was being gracious to him. Then when the opportunity arose, he communicated God's goodness to the Philippian jailer and brought him and his family to salvation. Likewise, James wrote, "Consider it all joy, my brethren, when you encounter various trials" (James 1:2).

Peace, I leave with you; my peace I give to you; not as the world gives, do I give to you. Let not your heart be troubled, nor let it be fearful. (John 14:27)

The peace Jesus is speaking of enables believers to remain calm in the most wildly fearful circumstances. It enables them to hush a cry, still a riot, rejoice in pain and trials, and sing in the middle of suffering. This peace is never by circumstances, but affects and even overrules them. (Excerpts from John MacArthur's article, The Gift of Peace)

Longsuffering… Having or showing patience despite troubles, especially those caused by other people. *What is longsuffering?* It is the Godly patience and mercy we need to show to others that mirrors as closely as possible the patience and mercy God shows to us.

It is when we bear with others, put up with their mistakes and inconsiderate actions, and truly forgive them for real or imagined offenses against us. It is enduring trials and waiting patiently and faithfully for God's intervention. As with all the other fruit of the Spirit, God wants us to be like him. God cares for all humanity; and he does it with tremendous compassion, mercy, and longsuffering. God's people are in training to become kings and priests to rule with him in the future (Revelation 1:6), and this involves learning to forgive others, to show mercy, and to be forbearing—or else we would be just like the worldly leaders of today.

Psalm 130:7 states: "O Israel, hope in the LORD; for with the LORD there is mercy, and with him is abundant redemption."

God set the example of mercy and redemption. God patiently waits (and has waited) for us as humans to repent and to stop destroying ourselves. God desires that we turn to him, and when we do, he even promises to help us overcome.

Longsuffering (meaning self-control or examination)

Here's a self-check list of questions to examine your condition

- Am I slow to wrath or quick to condemn?
- Do others describe me as calm and laid-back or impatient and easily offended?
- Does my patience with others mirror God's patience with me?
- Do I truly forgive others, or do I hold grudges? (Excerpts from Eddie Foster's Article on Fruit of the Spirit.

Gentleness… is the quality of being kind and careful. Your gentleness with a frightened stray dog will eventually convince her to let you feed and pet her. The noun gentleness is perfect for describing the way someone acts when they are soft and calm and sweet to other people.

Galatians 5:22-23 says that the Holy Spirit works in us to be more like Christ (Ephesians 4:14-16), and part of the fruit, or results, of that work is gentleness. Gentleness does not mean weakness. Rather, it involves humility and thankfulness toward God and polite, restrained behavior toward others. The opposites of gentleness are anger, a desire for revenge, and self-aggrandizement.

When we are filled with the Spirit's fruit of gentleness, we will correct others with easiness instead of arguing in resentment and anger, knowing that their salvation is far more important than our pride (II Timothy 24-25). We will forgive readily, because any offense toward us is nothing compared to our offenses against God—offenses he's already forgiven (Matthew 18:23-35). Competition and sectarianism will disappear, as the goal becomes less about ourselves and more about preaching the gospel (Philippians 1:15-18). John the Baptist was a fiery preacher, yet he evinced true gentleness when he said, "Jesus must become greater; I must become less" (John 3:30). (Taken from www.gotquestions?org)

Goodness… As the Holy Spirit works in our lives, our character changes. Where we had harbored selfishness, cruelty, rebelliousness, and spite, we now possess love, joy, peace, patience, kindness, goodness, faithfulness, gentleness, and self-control. Everything in the list reflects the character of God, and goodness is one that relates directly to morality.

Goodness is virtue and holiness in action. It results in a life characterized by deeds motivated by righteousness and a desire to be a blessing. It's a moral characteristic of a Spirit-filled person. The Greek word translated as "goodness," *agathosune*, is defined as "uprightness of heart and life." *Agathosune* is goodness for the benefit of others, not goodness simply for the sake of being virtuous.

Goodness is not a quality we can manufacture on our own. James 1:17 says, "Every good thing given and every perfect gift is from above, coming down from the Father of lights." This certainly includes a life characterized by goodness. By allowing the Holy Spirit to control us, we receive the blessing of the fruit of goodness. As others see our good works, they will praise our Father in heaven (Matthew 5:16).

Faith… Faithfulness is steadfastness, constancy, or allegiance; it is carefulness in keeping what we are entrusted with; it is the conviction that the scriptures accurately reflect reality.

Biblical faithfulness requires belief in what the Bible says about God—his existence, his works, and his character. Faithfulness is a fruit of the Spirit; it results from the Spirit working in us. But the Spirit is also our seal of faithfulness. He is our witness to God's promise that if we accept the truth about God, he will save us.

Hebrews 11 gives a long list of faithful men and women in the Old Testament who trusted God. Abel's understanding of God made his sacrifice real and authentic. Noah trusted God's word about the coming judgment and God's promise to save his family (Genesis 6-9).

Abraham and Sarah believed against all evidence that they would have a child (Genesis 21:1-34). Rahab trusted God to protect her family when the Israelites destroyed Jericho (Joshua 6). Gideon's mustard-seed faith routed an entire army (Judges 6-7).

In that list in Hebrews 11 is the example of Enoch, who "obtained the witness that before his being taken up, he was pleasing to God. And without faith it is impossible to please him, for he who comes to God must believe that he is, and that he is a rewarder of those who seek him" (vs. 5b-6). Faith, or a faithful commitment to who God says he is, is basic to walking with God. As Jesus traveled, he responded to people's faith and curtailed his involvement where there was no faith (Mark 6:1-6).

Faithfulness is believing that God is who he says he is and continuing in that belief despite those who object. Functionally, that means we trust what God says in the Bible, and not necessarily what the world or our own eyes tell us. We trust he will work out everything for good. We trust he will work his will in us, and we trust that our situation on earth is nothing compared to our future reward in heaven. The only way we can have such faith is by the Holy Spirit's influence. He testifies to the truth and impels us to seek God. The Spirit makes us faithful.

Meekness… There are two essential components for this quality to come into play in the Bible: a conflict in which an individual cannot control or influence circumstances. Typical human responses in such circumstances include frustration, bitterness, or anger, but the one who is guided by God's Spirit accepts God's ability to direct events (Gal. 5:23; Eph 4:2; Col 3:12; 1 Tim 6:11; Titus 3:2; James 1:21; 3:13).

Meekness is therefore an active and deliberate acceptance of undesirable circumstances that are wisely seen by the individual as only part of a larger picture. Meekness is not a resignation to fate or a passive and reluctant submission to events, for there is little virtue in such a response. Nevertheless, since the two responses and meekness are externally often indistinguishable, it is easy to see how what was once perceived as a virtue has become a defect in contemporary society.

The patient and hopeful endurance of undesirable circumstances identify the person as externally vulnerable and weak but inwardly resilient and strong. Meekness does not identify the weak but more precisely the strong that have been placed in a position of weakness where they persevere without giving up.

The use of the Greek word when applied to animals makes this clear, for it means "tame" when applied to wild animals. In other words, such animals have not lost their strength but have learned to control the destructive instincts that prevent them from living in harmony with man.

Therefore, it is quite appropriate for all people, from the poor to ancient Near Eastern kings, to describe their submission to God by the term "meek" (Moses in Num 12:3).. Nevertheless, in the incarnation, Jesus is freely described as meek, a concomitant of his submission to suffering and the will of the Father (Matt 11:29; 21:5; 2 Cor 10:1).

The single most frequently attested context in which the meek are mentioned in the Bible is one in which they are vindicated and rewarded for their patient endurance (Psalm 22:26; 25:9; 37:1; 76:9; 147:6; 149:4; Isa 11:4; 29:19; 61:1; Zeph 2:3; Matt 5:5).

Temperance… Many times, people think of the word "temperance" only in connection with alcohol. One might remember the "temperance" movement of the 20th Century, when this nation outlawed all alcohol from legal consumption for a time.

"Temperance" …. in the first century… The word "temperance" literally means regardless of what men today think about the term "temperance," (Strong's Hebrew/Greek Lexicon). In other words, studies and commentaries, we find similar definitions. J. H. Thayer said the word "temperance" means, "the virtue of one who masters his desires and passions, especially his sensual appetites" (New Greek- English Lexicon, p. 166-167). Mike Willis, in his commentary 5:23, on Galatians defines temperance as: "the dominion which one has over oneself or something…. the dominion that one has over his thoughts, words, and actions." (Truth Commentaries, The Book of Galatians, p. 271).

Other writers have expressed similar thoughts as well. Therefore, by combining what we have learned, we see that temperance involves the self-control of the mind or will and that it also encompasses keeping all words and actions under control. Specifically, God must hold control of the mind, mouth, and body through his word.

Therefore, while "temperance" can have reference to one not drinking alcohol (1 Peter 4:3-4), we see that the definition of temperance encompasses much more than not drinking. The term "temperance" influences all aspects of our lives as we learn to control our thoughts, words, and actions. As Paul said, "…bringing into captivity every thought to the obedience of Christ" (2 Corinthians 10:5). That is temperance!

Of course, the best way to determine the meaning of a Bible word is to examine it in a Biblical context and see how God used this word. The word "temperance" (as well as its various forms and tenses) is found six times in the King James Bible. We find its definition of "self-control" (and its various tenses) found eight times in the New King James Bible and

New American Standard. Let us look at some of the times temperance, or self-control, is used in the Bible and make some applications to ourselves.

The first mention of the word "temperance" (self-control) is found in Acts 24:25. In context, we read of Paul preaching to Felix and his wife Drusilla (Acts 24:24). Paul was in the custody of Felix because he was preaching the gospel, and in order to keep from being killed by the Jews, he appealed to Caesar., over forty Jews took an oath not to eat or drink until they had killed Paul (Acts 23:13-14).

When the chief captain heard of this plot, he sent Paul on to Felix, the governor with 200 soldiers, 70 horsemen, and 200 spearmen, and sent a letter to Felix telling him why Paul was being sent there (Acts 23:17-30). It is at this time that Paul had the opportunity to speak to Felix (Acts 24:24). The Bible says Felix "heard him concerning the faith in Christ." What did he hear? "He (Paul,) reasoned of righteousness, temperance, and judgment to come" (Acts 24:25). Paul obviously knew what this man needed to hear, and thus spoke to him concerning righteousness, i.e., God's will (Psalm 119:172; Romans 1:16-17), as well as self-control! In the Roman world, self-control (temperance) was almost unheard of.

Yet, they needed to control themselves in thought, word, and deed, as much as anyone today. Paul reasoned concerning the judgment as well, because "we must all appear before the judgment seat of Christ." We will one day stand before him to "receive rewards for the things done in his body, according to that he hath done, whether it be good or bad" (2 Corinthians 5:10). Felix's response was to tremble and send Paul away until he had a "convenient season." As far as we know, that season never arrived. Are we guilty of the same thing? Let us not put off the most important decision – saving our soul (Mark 16:16; Acts 2:38)!

In thinking about other occasions in which the Bible speaks of temperance (self-control) let us not forget that self-control is something that needs to be added to our faith. Looking to 2 Peter 1:5-8, we read, "And beside this, giving all diligence, add to your faith virtue; and to virtue knowledge; And to knowledge temperance; and to temperance patience; and to patience godliness; and to godliness brotherly kindness; and to brotherly kindness charity. For if these things be in you, and abound, they make you that ye shall neither be barren nor unfruitful in the knowledge of our Lord Jesus Christ."

This passage states the need for continued growth in the life of a Christian. His faith must increase, or grow, as he continues his journey as a Christian. Peter stresses the point of adding qualities to one's faith as he matures. Here, I hope we can understand the need to add temperance (self-control) to one's life. Without this control, how can we fight off temptations that come our way? How can we "resist the devil" (Jas. 4:7)? It cannot be done without self-control and the willingness to fight Satan as he tries to advance.

We read of another occasion calling for self-control when Paul wrote to the Corinthians. He wrote to encourage them in their service to the Lord. He said,

"Know ye not that they which run in a race run all, but one receives the prize? So run, that ye may obtain. And every man that strives for mastery is temperate in all things. Now they do it to obtain a corruptible crown, but we are incorruptible. I therefore so run, not as uncertainly; so fight I, not as one that beats the air: But I keep under my body, and bring it into subjection: lest that by any means, when I have preached to others, I myself should be a castaway" (1 Corinthians 9:24-27).

Here, Paul compares the life of the Christian to one competing in a sport (boxing v. 26, running v. 24); and the fact that in such sports, it requires patience, dedication, and control (being "temperate"). If we understand this when considering competing in athletics, how much more ought we to be self-controlled when it comes to obtaining the "incorruptible crown"?

Paul clarified that even he was not exempt from the admonition to be self-controlled. He said that he had to "keep under" (buffet, NAS; discipline, NKJ) his body lest he should be a castaway (disqualified). It was possible for Paul to lose in this race, just as it is possible for any other Christian. Therefore, he stresses the importance of self-control, holding fast, and seeing heaven at the end of this life. Yes, friends, without self-control (temperance) we will not see Heaven! (Article prepared by Jarrod Jacobs)

Nine fruits of the Spirit reveal the nature and character of God. However, as I said from the start, I believe Love is the only fruit, and all the other attributes listed above describe Love. So, if you want to know God, know that he is Love, (I John 4:8) and that love is revealed so you know what kind of love you are dealing with.

In today's society, love is everything else except what is defined here. It is self-seeking, self-centeredness, and self-absorbed. This type of love does not characterize God. However, the fruit of God's Spirit is what I call another "Reality Squared"

(The Gifts of The Holy Spirit)

Remember, we are moving from the flesh into the Spirit. Part of that move is to utilize the gifts of the Spirit that were given to the church for its edification. let us look deeper into his gifts. Remember what Paul told the church.

"Though I speak with the tongues of men and angels, and have not charity, I am become as sounding brass, or a tinkling cymbal. And though I have the gift of prophecy, and understand all mysteries and all knowledge; and though I have all faith, so that I could remove mountains and have not charity, I am nothing. And though I bestow all my goods to feed the poor, and though I give my body to be burned, and have not charity, it profits me nothing." I Corinthians 13:1-7

The obvious truth is that the gifts were to profit every believer. To do that, they needed to be administered, or operated, through the Spiritual fruits, in particular, LOVE.

Here are a few questions relative to these gifts ending with the death of the apostles.

- If, as we have seen, the gifts were for edification or profiting the church, why would God stop them? Wouldn't he want his church to be edified continually?
- The population of the world back then, when Jesus walked the earth, was approximately 300 million. Today it has exceeded 7 billion and is expected to top 9 billion in the next 5 years. It seems to me that the gifts are needed more today than ever before. Why would God cause them to cease when the population of planet Earth is exploding?
- We are living in the ***"End Times"*** where Satan is on the warpath against God's children, more so than ever before. Why would God stop the gifts of the Holy Spirit when we need them to fight against the wilds of the devil? (Especially the discerning of spirits, wisdom, etc.)
- The gifts were manifested to validate Jesus as the true Messiah. We need that just as much today as they did back then.

The answer, at least in my mind, is God did not stop the gifts. They are in operation today as before and are edifying the church, aiding the believer in his or her walk in these last days, validating the truth to those who see, and helping in the evangelism of a much bigger world than ever before.

That being said, let's look again at the gifts of the Spirit.

"Now there are diversities of gifts, but the same Spirit. And there are differences of administrations, but the same Lord. And there are diversities of operations, but it is the same God, which worketh all in all.

But the manifestation of the Spirit is given to every man to profit withal. For to one is given by the Spirit the word of wisdom; to another the word of knowledge by the same Spirit; To another faith by the same Spirit; to another the gifts of healing by the same Spirit; To another the working of miracles; to another prophecy; to another discerning of spirits; to another divers kinds of tongues; to another the interpretation of tongues: But all these worketh that one and the selfsame Spirit, dividing to every man severally as he will." I Corinthians 12:7-11

This passage of scripture informs us that the Spirit gives the manifestation to every person for their edification and the benefit of all. The Holy Spirit manifests himself through the gifts. The Holy Spirit spreads out the gifts so that everyone has several, but no one has them all.

I Corinthians 12

The Word of Wisdom… A good definition of the word wisdom is the supernatural ability to apply knowledge the right way. This gift can be verbal but it is not considered a gift of utterance. We can receive a word of wisdom and keep silent unlike a message in tongues and interpretation or a message of prophecy. Usually, we will, at the right time, share the word of wisdom. This word can come from a dream, revelation, a vision, some have heard the audible voice of God, but usually, it is the still small voice of the Holy Spirit speaking to our spirit.

The Word of Knowledge… A divine gift at the will of the Holy Spirit giving someone certain facts from the mind of God. It is only a word, and it is supernatural. The person does not have to be naturally gifted in wisdom or knowledge. This gift is supernatural. The giving of this gift is spontaneous and does not follow a planned schedule. We cannot just decide before coming to church that we are going to receive a word of knowledge. It is according to the will of the Spirit and not our own will.

Faith… The definition of faith, according to the Bible, is the "substance of things hoped for and the evidence of things not seen with our natural eyes." It is something we all should develop and possess as we read the word and communicate with our Father in heaven. The gift of faith, though, is still a little different. It is the supernatural manifestation of the Holy Spirit that places the assurance of an answer to a certain prayer in our hearts at a certain point in time. It is like the gift of knowledge in that when this occurs, we know ahead of time supernaturally that what we prayed for is going to happen. This is not guesswork. When we receive this gift of faith at a certain time, whatever our spirit is saying will happen, will most certainly occur.

Gifts of Healing… There are gifts of healing, meaning multiple. The purpose is to prove that the word of God we preach and teach is true. It proves the power of the resurrection of Jesus Christ. We must never major on any gift and remove it from the foundation of Jesus Christ because the main reason for all nine gifts is to prove that all need to be born again by the spirit to be saved and that Jesus is the only way of salvation. Signs follow to prove what we say is true. The Holy Spirit brings people to Jesus and then we are to disciple others to bring more people to Jesus. We must not be moved away from that foundation. Jesus is the foundation.

The Working of Miracles… The working of miracles occurs as the will of the Holy Spirit at the right time, when and where he wills. We do not just decide that we are going to have a miracle today. In fact, all nine gifts work this same way. Miracles bring glory to God, bring the lost to the saving knowledge of Jesus Christ, and demonstrate with visible outward signs the truth of God's word. It is to convince unbelievers that God's word is true, Jesus is truly the way of salvation and the only way to God, and that what we are speaking and teaching is true. It is not to glorify men and cause men to be in control of a group of people. It is not to show off or use as a sideshow for the gift itself. The gift is to glorify the Lord.

6. Prophecy…… Prophecy is to speak for God, from the mind of God. It is an inspired word, usually short in duration but can be longer. It is a vocal utterance in one's own language that is understood by all present. It is like the interpretation of tongues, but no tongues precede it. Tongues and an interpretation are equal to a word of prophecy. The purpose for the gift of prophecy is in 1 Corinthians 14:3 "But he that prophesies, speaks unto men to edification, and exhortation and comfort."

7. Discerning of Spirits… Those of us who have this gift have been given the ability to discern spirits. They fall into these categories: the spirit of the Antichrist, the spirit of God, the spirit of the flesh, lying spirits, and the spirits of evil that bring infirmities, sickness, and disease. The believer can usually look at a person and discern what spirit they are of.

8. Various Kinds of Tongues… A language spoken somewhere in the world or in heaven either in the past or at present. Some call it a heavenly language. However, I have heard languages that sound like French, Arabic, Italian, Hebrew, Russian, and Vietnamese. It is a fluent language complete with accents. Not all experiences are the same, so I say this with caution, not to make anyone feel that if their experience is not like I describe, it means that something is not right.

9. The Interpretation of Tongues… A supernatural manifestation comes at the will of the Holy Spirit to give meaning to a message one has previously spoken verbally in tongues or another language as the spirit of God gave the utterance. Both the tongues and the interpretation are spontaneous, unplanned, and by the will of the Holy Spirit. Like all the gifts of the spirit, we do not plan ahead of time that we are going to have a message in tongues or an interpretation of tongues. All supernatural gifts of the Holy Spirit are unexpected, unplanned, and spontaneous, just like the coming of the Lord is going to be. Maybe these things prepare us for that great event.

So, there are nine gifts of the Holy Spirit and when you see them in operation, you see a manifestation of the Holy Spirit in your midst.

Here are a few points to remember concerning the gifts:

- Gifts will never contradict the written word of God.
- Gifts will always be presented in an orderly fashion.
- Gifts will always glorify Jesus.
- Gifts will never exhaust any individual.

Which is the best gift? I believe that the best gift is the one that is needed to do the job at the time you need it. If you need healing and someone says, "I Have The Interpretation of Tongues", that gift will not do the job. You will need the "Gifts of Healing."

Most Christians are familiar with the nine gifts of the Spirit mentioned above, that Paul describes in 1 Corinthians 12:4-10. But did you know there are many more? Though the exact number is debatable, here are at least 15 more spiritual gifts the Holy Spirit gave to the early church—and continues to give today. (Presented by Charisma Magazine)

- Helping (1 Cor. 12:28)
- Administration (1 Cor. 12:28; Acts 6:2-3)
- Ministry/service (Rom. 12:7; 2 Tim. 1:16-18)
- Teaching (Rom. 12:7; Eph. 4:11-14)
- Encouragement (Rom. 12:8; Heb. 10:24-25)
- Giving (Rom. 12:8; 1 Cor. 13:3; Acts 4:32-35)
- Leadership (Rom. 12:8; Acts 13:12)
- Mercy (Rom. 12:8; Luke 5:12-13)
- Apostleship (Eph. 4:11)
- Evangelism (Eph. 4:11; 2 Tim. 4:5)
- Pastoral guidance (Eph. 4:11)
- Grace (Rom. 12:6; Eph. 3:7; 4:7; 1 Pet. 4:10-11)
- Willingness to face martyrdom (1 Cor. 13:3)
- Intercession (Rom. 8:26-27)
- Hospitality (1 Pet. 4:9)

The first nine gifts presented by Paul are supernatural and operate independently from the "Fee Will" of man. Though he may have a certain level of control over the gift, he does not require pre-training to participate. He is a vessel through which the gift flows.

The remaining fifteen gifts are subject to man's will to participate or not and usually require some sort of pre-training. These gifts operate in a joint effort between Spirit and man, whereas, the first nine gifts operate exclusively at the pleasure of the Holy Spirit.

The fruit of the Spirit is automatically given to the believer when he or she gets saved. "Walking in the Spirit" is how the world sees Jesus in you. Godly fruit is manifested in us. Change occurs so a Godly personality shines through. Staying in the Spirit will bring the image and likeness of God into the earth through the lifestyle of the believer.

The nine gifts of the Spirit spoken of here come to the believer through a "Baptism of the Holy Ghost" that is separate from the salvation baptism. Being filled with the Spirit refers to the gifts. Being "Anointed" for ministry through the Spirit baptism refers to receiving one or more of the nine Holy Spirit gifts.

Both fruit and gifts are available to those who desire a closer walk with Jesus and deeper communication with God. It is the language of the Spirit in the reality of God.

Isn't it wonderful to see God at work in our lives? His fruit transforms us into his image and likeness. His gifts open the door for evangelism and body ministry.

God has seen fit to partner with us to overcome the wiles of the devil and take back what has been stolen from us. The gifts and the fruits make us the "Head" and not the "Tail." We are the children of God.

It is high time to put aside the things of this world and be filled with the Spirit. It is high time to seek spiritual gifts and learn how to operate in them. You could be the one person that God has been waiting for to stand up and be counted among the children of God.

Now let us discuss actually walking in the Spirit

We are commanded to walk in the Spirit of God. The purpose of this command is so we will not fulfill the lust of the flesh. Listen to what was spoken to the 1st century Christians: "This I say then,"(Paul said), "Walk in the Spirit, and ye shall not fulfill the lust of the flesh" (Galatians 5:16). Then again, "if we live in the Spirit, let us also walk in the Spirit" (Galatians 5:25).

Although they appear to be the same command in English, there is a significant distinction in the original Greek language in which Paul penned the letters.

Both the Romans 8:1 and the Galatians 5:16 passages use the word *perepeto*, which carries the connotation to "walk around" and to "be at liberty."

The second iteration in Galatians 5:25 uses *stoicheo*, which means to "step precisely," to "march," or to "go in procession." Same command but a different emphasis. (Excerpts from an article by Henry M. Morris III, D. Min. Institute For Creation Research)

Using two different words tells me that we have the liberty to hang around with God in his Spirit to fellowship with him, but we also must walk precisely along the path he has shown us to achieve victory.

As a young Christian, I often wondered what it meant to walk in God's Holy Spirit. I was also curious to know how to live in the Spirit. Was there a set of rules? How does one live and walk in the Spirit of the living God? Is it possible? As I grew in Bible knowledge, it all became clear to me. I have to admit that it is still hard sometimes to stay in the Spirit and even walk in him because the devil is hard after me to walk in the flesh. I falter now and then.

Galatians 5 offers a contrast between a lifestyle of fleshly behavior and a life controlled by the Holy Spirit. The "deeds" of the flesh and the "fruit" of the Spirit stand in complete opposition to each other. They continually fight for control of our minds to manifest their image here on the earth through us. However, they cannot exist together; they are not co-rulers.

(Romans 8:5-8) We either "mind" the things of the flesh or the "things of the Spirit." (Romans 8:5)

Only, "Born Again" Folk Can Walk In The Spirit

I'll bet you didn't know that you cannot be or live in neutrality. We are created beings by God for one primary purpose…to reveal his image upon the earth. The original plan was that humanity would live and walk in the Spirit on this earth as a reflection of God. To see us would be like seeing God because we looked just like him. "So, God created man in his own image, in the image of God created he him; male and female created he them." Genesis 1:27.

However, sin entered the world and replaced the image of God with the image of Satan. (Romans 5:12) Mankind now is ruled by evil instead of good. His nature and character reveal the sin that reigns in his heart. He has no choice but to live out this evil destiny.

All that God wanted for humanity was lost because man no longer dwelt in the Spirit of God. Even his love became distorted and his whole reasoning fell into a selfish gratification. God's race of Godly children, fashioned in his own likeness, was lost, seemingly forever. Man became a distortion of mind and body that led to a worldwide flood, a sentence of death for all who are called human after Adam's kind. "For all have sinned, and come short of the glory of God" Romans 3:23

God's Plan of Redemption

But God did not leave man in such a depraved state with no choice. He honored his plan for the ages which was to allow man to have a "Free Will" and to be his own free moral agent. His Lordship over man would not be evil but righteous as he restored man to a status of being able, once again, to walk in his Spirit. The choice was given back to man. He can now choose to live in sin or walk in the righteousness of God.

We also know that it was God who designed this plan of redemption and set it in motion, even before the foundation of the world. That plan was

Christ crucified, once and for all, that whosoever believes in him, this Jesus of Nazareth, who died as a penalty for sin, who was made sin for us, would not perish but have everlasting life. (Ephesians 1:4, John 3:16, II Corinthians 5:21)

So, only those who accept God's plan of salvation have the choice of walking in his Spirit. Those who do not believe and do not accept the gift of salvation through faith are bound by their evil nature to live out a destiny that is the image and likeness of Satan.

Two Natures In Conflict

"For the flesh lusts against the Spirit, and the Spirit against the flesh: and these are contrary the one to the other: so that ye cannot do the things that ye would." (Galatians 5:17) We, that is, us Christians, are constantly being offered a choice. We can select the fruit of God's Spirit or the works of the flesh.

Galatians 5:22 describes the fruit and the works. "But the fruit of the Spirit is love, joy, peace, longsuffering, gentleness, goodness, faith, Meekness, temperance: against such there is no law."

Galatians 5:19-21 told us what the works of the flesh are, "Now the works of the flesh are manifest, which are these; adultery, fornication, uncleanness, lasciviousness, idolatry, witchcraft, hatred, variance, emulations, wrath, strife, seditions, heresies, envying, murders, drunkenness, revellings, and such like: of the which I tell you before, as I have also told you in time past, that they which do such things shall not inherit the kingdom of God.

Now here's the kicker…" And they that are Christ's have crucified the flesh with the affections and lusts." Galatians 5:24

We crucify the flesh by denying it access to our emotions. We put it to death by not allowing it to be manifested in us. We will still get angry, but we do not allow that anger to be released. Instead, we focus on the fruit of God's Spirit to overcome the flesh, thus filling ourselves with the image and likeness of God. Instead of getting angry, we pray for and demonstrate longsuffering and love.

How Do We Walk In This New Nature?

The phrase "walk in the Spirit" occurs not only in Galatians chapter five, verse 25 but also in verse 16, "But I say, walk in the Spirit and do not gratify the desires of the flesh." So here we see what the opposite of walking by the Spirit is, namely, giving in to the desires of the flesh.

Remember, "flesh" is the ordinary human nature that does not relish the things of God and prefers to get satisfaction from a sinful lifestyle. When we "walk in the Spirit," those things do not control us. This is what verse 17 means: the flesh produces one kind of desire, and the Spirit produces another and they are opposed or contrary to each other.

Paul said in Romans 7:18, "I know that in me, that is, in my flesh, dwells no good thing." He also said "for the mind of the flesh is hostile to God's law and does not submit to it because it cannot." (Romans 8:7)

The "New Birth" creates a whole new array of desires that want to please God. Therefore, "walking in the Spirit" is something the Holy Spirit enables us to do by producing in us strong desires that are in accord with God's will. This is what God said he would do in Ezekiel 36:26, 27: "A new heart I will give you and a new spirit I will put within you . . . I will put my Spirit within you and cause you to walk in my statutes." Thus, when we "walk in the Spirit," we experience the fulfillment of this prophecy.

The Big Question

This brings up a big question in my mind that you too may have asked: Do I just sit back and wait for new desires before I can walk in the Spirit? Of course not!

"And be not drunk with wine, wherein is excess; but be filled with the Spirit; Speaking to yourselves in psalms and hymns and spiritual songs, singing and making melody in your heart to the Lord; Giving thanks always for all things unto God and the Father in the name of our Lord Jesus Christ" Ephesians 5:18-20.

There are several things we need to do to establish and continue our walk in the Spirit. I offer these as a starting point for your consideration:

- **Pray to be filled with the Spirit**… "And be not drunk with wine, wherein is excess; but be filled with the Spirit." Ephesians 5:18

Then do what Ephesians says…The more we sing, make melody, read psalms, and pray, the longer we stay filled. When our thoughts are on the things of the Lord, they cannot be dwelling on the things of the flesh. Some folks refer to this action as ***"Practicing The Presence of God."***

- **Have no confidence in the flesh**… "For we are the circumcision, which worship God in the spirit, and rejoice in Christ Jesus, and have no confidence in the flesh. Though I might also have confidence in the flesh" Philippians 3:3 (The Flesh is the unregenerate man that is led by Satan via a nature of sin

When we have no confidence in the flesh, we do not put any faith in our own decision-making power. We always consult the Lord first about what to do in any situation. We do not rely on our emotions.

- **Resist The devil and he will flee from you**…Be sober, be vigilant; because your adversary the devil, as a roaring lion, walketh about, seeking whom he may devour: I Peter 5:8-9

When we resist the devil, we are resisting his many and different temptations to operate independently from God. He wants us to live in the flesh because it is his nature and we will, if we do so, manifest the image and likeness of Satan, the evil one. Thus, the purpose of his temptations is to keep us from walking in the Spirit.

- **Walk By Faith**…" For we walk by faith, not by sight" (II Corinthians 5:7

When we walk by faith, we walk in the promises of God that are given to us in the Bible. We live in them. If God said it, we will believe it and apply it in our lives. We will hold on to every word, knowing that God will cause every promise he has spoken into our spirits to come true. This keeps us free from all distractions that would lead us away from walking in the Spirit.

Spiritual Breathing

By Bill Bright of Campus Crusade for Christ

The Christian life, properly understood, is not complex nor is it difficult. The Christian life is very simple. It is so simple that we stumble over the very simplicity of it, and yet it is so difficult that no one can live it!

This paradox occurs because the Christian life is a supernatural life. The only one who can help us live this abundant life is the Lord Jesus Christ, who empowers us with His Holy Spirit.

One of the most important truths of Scripture, the understanding and application of which has enriched my life as has no other truth, is a concept which I like to call **"Spiritual Breathing."** This concept has been shared with millions–with revolutionary results–through our literature and various training conferences and seminars.

As you walk in the Spirit by faith, practicing "Spiritual Breathing", you need never again live in spiritual defeat. "Spiritual Breathing", like physical breathing, is a process of exhaling the impure and inhaling the pure, an exercise in faith that enables you to experience God's love and forgiveness and walk in the Spirit as a way of life. (*You breath in the Word of God and you exhale the negative destructive emotions*)

The moment you invited Christ into your life as Savior and Lord, you experienced a spiritual birth. Inviting Christ into your life as Savior and Lord resulted in you becoming a child of God and being filled with the Holy Spirit. God forgave your sins–past, present, and future–making you righteous, holy, and acceptable in his sight because of Christ's sacrifice for you on the cross. You received the power to live a holy life and be a fruitful witness for God.

If this is your experience, "Spiritual Breathing" will enable you to get off this emotional roller coaster and enjoy the Christian life that the Lord Jesus promised to you when He said, *"I came that they might have life and might have it abundantly."* John 10:10 As an exercise in faith, "Spiritual Breathing" will make it possible for you to continue to experience God's love, forgiveness, and the power of the Holy Spirit as a way of life.

If you try to live the Christian life by your own fleshly effort, it becomes complex, difficult, and even impossible to live. But when you invite the Lord Jesus to direct your life; when you know the reality of having been crucified with Christ and raised with him by faith as a way of life; when you walk in the light as God is in the light in the fullness and power of the Holy Spirit, the Lord Jesus simply lives his abundant life within you in all his resurrection power.

I'm not suggesting that the Christian who walks in the fullness of the Spirit will have no difficulties. Problems of poor health, loss of loved ones, financial needs and other such experiences are common to all people. However, many of our misfortunes are self-imposed because of our own worldly, selfish actions.

The spiritual person avoids most of these self-imposed hardships. But when the problems do come, the spiritual person can face them with a calm, confident attitude because he is aware of God's resources, which are available to him to deal with adversity. (Excerpts from Bill Bright's article from The Power to Change)

Being Continually Filled

The command of Ephesians 5:18 is given to all believers to be filled, directed, and empowered by the Holy Spirit. Being filled with the Holy Spirit, however, is a continuous experience. In the Greek language in which this command was originally written, the meaning is clearer than that in most English translations. This command of God means to be constantly and continually filled, controlled,, and empowered with the Holy Spirit as a way of life.

If you look at the scripture from verses 15-18 you see a truth that few have understood. See if you see what I see.

"See then that ye walk circumspectly, not as fools, but as wise, redeeming the time, because the days are evil. Wherefore be ye not unwise, but understanding what the will of the Lord is. And be not drunk with wine, wherein is excess; but be filled with the Spirit; Speaking to yourselves in psalms and hymns and spiritual songs, singing and making melody in your heart to the Lord; Giving thanks always for all things unto God and the Father in the name of our Lord Jesus Christ." Galatians 5:15-20.

Here is what I see:

- We are to use wisdom and not to be fools. In doing so, we can redeem the time lost to the past in living in sin.
- We are not to drink in excess, but in contrast to that lifestyle; we are to be continually filled with God's Spirit. This is the will of the Lord.
- The way we keep ourselves filled with the Spirit is to sing, make melody in our hearts, and give thanks to our Heavenly Father in the name of Jesus.

The process of praise, prayer, and reading the psalms will keep you from the flesh and drunkenness. It will also continually fill you with the Spirit. We receive faith by reading the Word. We are filled with joy by singing. We are blessed with peace by giving thanks. It all comes together inside of us to continually keep us in the Spirit.

Note: Some have said that we leak and the spirit, like water, drains out of us. This is nothing more than foolishness. We are faced with a choice in life, to dwell in the flesh and ride the emotional roller coaster… or to be filled with the Spirit and walk in peace with God through this upside-down world.

Back And Forth

We can, however, fall back into the flesh. Paul wrote to the Galatians and said, "O foolish Galatians, who hath bewitched you, that ye should not obey the truth, before whose eyes Jesus Christ hath been evidently set forth, crucified among you? This only would I learn of you, received ye the Spirit by the works of the law, or by the hearing of faith? Are ye so foolish, having begun in the Spirit, are ye now made perfect by the flesh?" Galatians 3:1-3.

The Galatians started in the Spirit but somehow believed a lie and went back into the works of the law, which opposed the grace of God. Paul called them foolish. This example shows how the devil can lead you away from the truth and cause you to operate in the flesh. That is how he defeats Christians. He spins a lie and we get confused and end up believing it and eventually, it changes our thinking.

Remember, non-believers do not have two natures. They can only operate in the flesh. Seeing the state of our current society with so much evil, the flesh is running rampant.

However, we are blessed with a new nature that is holy and righteous in every way. It is the same nature of Jesus and the very likeness of God. It is his image. We can choose the new, reject the old and walk in his Spirit. This is a benefit of the "New Birth" experience when we are "Born Again."

Some Hindrances

When we strive to walk with God and fellowship with him, the devil always attacks us because the devil does not want us to do that. He wants us in the flesh so he can torment us. However, he cannot even get to us when we are *"In The Spirit."* He must draw us away with some sort of temptation or lie.

Let's look at a few hindrances.

Fear of Rejection…" But God forbid that I should glory, save in the cross of our Lord Jesus Christ, by whom the world is crucified unto me, and I unto the world." Gal. 6:14.

In the above scripture, I find that the cross is the mark of distinction between the world and me. Sometimes I hear people say, "I want to walk with God, but I don't know how I could never give up my friends." My answer to that is very simple: If you walk with the Lord, you won't have to worry about giving up your friends; you won't have time for that--they will give you up first. That is how the cross is a mark of distinction.

Living by your feelings and not by faith…As we have already said, living in the flesh is living by your feelings. It offers only a terrifying ride on that emotional roller coaster.

Failure in simple obedience…Again we look to Galatians where Paul told the church, "Ye did run well; who did hinder you that ye should not obey the truth?" Disobedience will always stop the flow of God's anointing and kick us out of His Spirit, and back into the flesh.

Allowing others to hinder you…Again in Galatians, it was someone or many that hindered the church from obeying the truth. We cannot allow others to sway us from the truth.

Giving in to temptation…Temptation will do it every time. It will cause you to fall if you give in to it. Paul, in Galatians 3:1 said, "Oh foolish Galatians" He knew they had given into the pressures and expectations of others. Their desire to be politically correct was stronger than their desire to obey the truth. We can never give in.

Seeing What's Not Visible

As I mentioned before, the Christian has two natures and must choose one or the other. Both natures will clamor for attention and the chance for expression. One is Holy and the other is evil.

This evil nature has polluted our souls, invaded our DNA, and dominated our emotions. Its rule over us is cruel. Its goal is to manifest wickedness as a lifestyle and image.

The holy nature is newly fashioned as a "Born Again" experience, where we repent of our sins and put our faith in Jesus. Its goal is to manifest the fruit of God's Spirit through a gentle Lordship where we can be blessed and live an abundant life.

Because we have the dominant nature of evil ruling, we see life through its eyes and process events on an emotional level. The new nature of holiness is equally capable of sight but looks only into the spirit realm. It sees and discerns spiritual things. It processes events based on the Will of God and the believer's divine destiny.

Most Christians see only with their human nature, which relies on its emotions. Seeing with Spiritual eyes is different. The holy nature in you relies on divine revelation from its creator. The result is divine wisdom that enhances our ability to make Godly decisions. You cannot walk in the Spirit without seeing in the Spirit. The eyes of the Spirit are the scriptures. It is there that our eyes are opened and our focus made clear.

Now that you kind of know about how the two natures operate in us when called upon, it is important to realize that there is another, "Free Will" choice to be made…which nature to call upon. We are bent on the evil nature. Holiness is contrary to our natural feel. To allow it to advise and control our decisions is not automatic. That is why we are encouraged to deny the flesh by crucifying it with all its lust and evil affections. We must deny the evil to live in the Holy/Spiritual nature.

When we are faced with a situation or happening, we automatically decide on what to do. As a man, I am often confronted with women crossing my path or coming into my line of sight. If my human nature is ruling, my emotions will spike and I will most likely fall into some sort of fantasy. If, on the other hand, my holy nature is in control, I automatically hear the scriptures speaking in my head telling me what the "Word of God" said about the situation and what I need to do to stay in the Spirit.

If you do not know the scriptures, you will walk as a blind man and cannot discern the times you live in, the snares of the devil, the demonic temptations that, as fiery darts, are hurled at you, and the many day-to-day decisions that fill your life.

The psalmist said, "Thy word have I hid in mine heart, that I might not sin against thee." Psalm 119:11 Without the hiding of "God's Word" in your heart, you have nothing to draw from to make a holy decision. You are blind and usually fall back into the human nature that once ruled your life and wrecked your emotions.

The Christian walk has great liberty (Romans 8:21), but that liberty must "step precisely" in honesty (Romans 13:13), good works (Ephesians 2:10), and in truth (2 John 4-6).

Our walk is expected to be by faith and not by sight (2 Corinthians 5:7) We are to conduct spiritual warfare in the Holy Spirit's power (2 Corinthians 10:3-5) We are to protect ourselves by putting on the full armor of God (Ephesians 6:10-18).

However, the most important thing to remember is that we need to stay in the Spirit and we can only do that by reading the scriptures to gain faith, singing, and making melody in our hearts unto the Lord and giving thanks to our heavenly Father in the name of Jesus. That keeps us in the Spirit.

Walking in the Spirit is another "Reality Squared" event. God designs it to lift us onto his level so he can communicate with us and fellowship with us, spirit to Spirit, as it was originally intended.

May our Lord bless you as you walk with him.

CHAPTER FOUR:
"HOW TO" AVOID THE MULTIPLICITY FACTOR

Multiple Choices, Multiple Realities, & Multiple Destinies

Attaining and enjoying the reality of God will also require avoiding certain things. Life is full of different realities and man is full of "Free Will" choices. He can do whatever he wants when he wants, and for any reason. He is a "Free Moral Agent" endowed by God at creation.

The problem with being free to select any course of action is that man does not know what is best. I can remember when I was about to graduate high school. many of us seniors did not have a clue what to do next. Some would say, "I am going to be a doctor, while others boasted about becoming a lawyer. Still others went into the military. All the girls wanted to get married and have babies. This was my generation…groping in the dark for something, but not knowing what.

As time marched on, we went to college, had babies, changed jobs several times, and tried to find ourselves in our work. We identified ourselves by what we did for a living and judged each other's social status by how much money and influence we had. Then we found out that life would not last forever, so we retired and drifted into the status of a "has-been." (Different realities at different stages of life)

Along the way, we struggled to find a reason to live and a destiny to achieve. Being rich, famous, or having power seemed to have lost its luster. When you are pushing 80 and going from doctor to doctor, all that worldly stuff just does not matter anymore.

However, there is a "Multiplicity" factor that is evident in living life on planet Earth. This factor is seen in repeats, such as wives, jobs, actions, neighborhoods, churches, and even thoughts. It is mostly seen in the "Do-overs" of life. How many of us are still with the wife of our youth? Statistics show about 50%. Who is still living in the same neighborhood where you grew up? How many times did you change jobs over the years?

My point is…There is a "Multiplicity" going on in our lives that is caused by our own choices. This multiplicity of "Free Will" choices has caused our destiny to change many times. Most of us can say, "I was and now I am" but tomorrow has yet to be determined. We can avoid this process of multiplicity by making good choices. Only God can know what choices are good and what choices are not.

Each time we make a decision, no matter how small or large, our destiny changes. If I decide to step out on my wife to be with another, I go from a faithful husband to an unfaithful and immoral jerk. The decision takes me into guilt, fear of getting caught, and most likely divorce. My reality changes and my destiny changes. So it is with almost every other aspect of life. There is a cause and effect or result to every action we do. Sometimes, it is down the road of life but it will still catch up with you. Hear it from a Biblical perspective.

"Be not deceived; God is not mocked: for whatsoever a man soweth, that shall he also reap." Galatians 6:7 (Sow = planting & Reap = harvesting)

God does not let us get away with anything. We may think we did but God will bring it back in many ways that most of the time take us into an alternate reality and a shift into a different destiny. A good example is the man who was caught robbing a grocery store.

After his court date and trial before a Judge, he is sent to prison to pay for his crime. His reality is now in a prison cell among worse criminals.

His destiny has been shut down for so many years or months. His choice to commit a robbery planted a seed that quickly grew into a harvest of sorrow, punishment, fear, and a loss of freedom.

What does all of this have to do with "Reality Squared?" Let me explain further. A thief never just steals one time. Once a thief, always a thief… unless the thief repents and gets "Born Again" which will change his direction in life. The actions of a thief are repeated in burglary after burglary. There is a "Multiplicity" factor that sets the destiny of the thief. He is going down the wrong path in life and eventually will reap the harvest.

Here is a Biblical example that might make more sense.

"I call heaven and earth to record this day against you, *that* I have set before you life and death, blessing and cursing: therefore, choose life, that both thou and thy seed may live:" Deuteronomy 30:19

Can you see the two destinies in the above scripture? They are "Life or Death;" "Blessing or Cursing." Can you see who benefits or not from the choice made? They are the adults that will choose and the offspring that will suffer or be blessed because of their parent's choices. Your choices can change the destiny of your children.

When we move into a sinful act, we activate the "Multiplicity Factor." The odds of repeating that act are great. We acted upon the fault because of our lust and the lust does not go away unless we repent and become filled with God's Spirit. His control will keep us from "Do-Overs" that are rooted in the "Flesh." Walk in the Spirit and you will not experience the flesh and avoid the multiplicity factor. "Do-Overs" will not be necessary.

Remember, we are looking for a pathway to the reality of God, where we can be blessed and accepted. We can choose life and not fall prey to evil forces, false assumptions, and bad choices. We want to learn from our mistakes and align our thoughts to the will of God so we can have a good life here and a destiny that takes us into the kingdom of God for all of eternity.

CHAPTER FIVE:
"HOW TO" MASTER SPIRITUAL SELF-DEFENSE

Fighting The Good Fight of Faith

In this chapter, we will look at the reality of evil and learn what we can do to overcome it. Remember, our goal is to find the pathway to the reality of God, where we can live and have our being. This is what I call "Reality Squared."

As believers in Christ and his followers, we must be cognizant of the wiles of the devil. He is determined to defeat us with our own words. He has no power of his own. He must deceive us into making decisions that will change our reality into what he wants instead of what God wants.

When was the last time you got into a fight? Was it a knockdown, drag-out battle, or just a few punches? Most of us are gentle and avoid physical contact, intending to do bodily harm. We just want to be left alone to do our own thing. ***"Live and let live"*** is our motto. Anger and violence are not a normal part of our daily routine.

So why all the hoopla about having to fight? What is all this noise about this good fight of faith? I do not hurt anybody and I do not practice evil. Who is it that wants to hurt me? That type of thinking just makes no sense.

If that is what you think and the way you feel, good luck in getting through life without going crazy. I heard a sermon the other day where the minister said that 75% of illnesses in America stem from an emotional disorder. Folks are going crazy and do not know why.

It is impossible to be neutral in a war that is aimed at your destruction. There is no negotiating with the enemy. Compromise only leads you further down the road to hell and eternal destruction. If you are human, of the Adamic race, you are marked for torment and death by an unseen enemy that God tossed out of his kingdom ages ago.

However, there is hope. Jesus loves you and gave you his Holy Spirit to dwell in you and guide you into all truth so you can live in freedom apart from visible or unseen enemies.

Evil spirits will not rule over you if you join Jesus in *"The Good Fight of Faith."* Your mindset needs to change from "Me, Myself and I" to focusing on God's will and his teaching on how to fight against his and your enemies.

We will look at the battle, the enemy, the weapons, the war perspective, and other related tools you can use to keep yourself out of harm's way. This is what I call "Spiritual, Self-Defense."

First, you need to know who your enemy is. I have covered most of this in previous chapters, but I feel a quick summary is in order. The apostle, Paul told us that, *"For we wrestle not against flesh and blood, but against principalities, against powers, against the rulers of the darkness of this world, against spiritual wickedness in high places."* Ephesians 6:12.

Surprise! People are not our enemy. Our fight is with evil spiritual forces. They will surely attack us through people but our fight is not with them. We need to stand in faith and use the word of God to overcome. Check out I Peter 5:8-9.

Second, you will need the armor of God, not your own. I have discussed this before. You can find the full armor and how it works in Ephesians 6:10-20.

Guess What? The shield of faith is your greatest defense and your best offensive weapon because it quenches the "Fiery Darts" of the enemy.

Third, be battle-ready for the mind games played by evil forces and use the spoiler, II Corinthians 10:4-9, to keep stray thoughts from forming strongholds in your mind. You can win the battle that rages in your mind by bringing every thought into the obedience of God and casting down all that exalts itself above the knowledge of God. Because the battle takes place in your mind, this is a great way to spoil the attack and stop the fiery darts.

Fourth, use the "Peace of God" as a weapon. Let it be the referee in every circumstance. You can walk in his peace and if you fall, his peace will leave you and you will know right away that you are off sides.

Fifth, walk in the Spirit and you will not fulfill the lust of the flesh.

Marching Orders! God gives us marching orders that help us to arrive safely. They are written in promises and holy revelations in the Bible. You will need to look for them, study them, and walk in them if you are to succeed.

The Bible tells us that our battle is a "Good Fight" because we are fighting a defeated enemy. He has no power unless he steals it from us. We are the head and he is the tail. All we have to do is stand in faith, resist him and watch him flee.

Good will always overcome evil because good is the nature of God and God never loses. At the end of the day, God wins.

Nevertheless, we are in a life-and-death struggle with the forces of evil. Our destiny depends upon how we fight and live our lives here on this earth. The forces of evil can take the unsaved at their own will because they are children of darkness, but the "Born Again" believer is washed in the blood of Christ and has the Holy Spirit of promise inside of him or her. He or she can overcome. Here are the support scriptures to prove what I am saying.

The Seal of Promise… "Who hath also sealed us, and given the earnest of the Spirit in our hearts." 11 Corinthians 1:22 "In him you also, when you heard the word of truth, the gospel of your salvation, and believed in him, were sealed with the promised Holy Spirit, who is the guarantee of our inheritance until we acquire possession of it, to the praise of his glory." Ephesians 1:13.

The Holy Spirit is God's seal on his people, his claim on us as his very own. The Greek word translated as "earnest" in these passages is *arrhabōn* which means "a pledge," that is, part of the purchase of money or property given in advance as security for the rest. The gift of the Spirit to believers is a down payment on our heavenly inheritance, which Christ has promised us and secured for us at the cross. It is because the Spirit has sealed us that we are assured of our salvation. No one can break the seal of God.

The Greater Spirit… "Ye are of God, little children, and have overcome them: because greater is he that is in you than he that is in the world." 1 John 4:4 "But ye are not in the flesh, but in the Spirit, if so be that the Spirit of God dwell in you. Now if any man has not the Spirit of Christ, he is none of his." Romans 8:9

The Holy Spirit is inside of us guiding us and leading us along the narrow path to glory. His counsel is greater than any evil spirit that attacks our souls from without. However, "when he, the Spirit of truth, is come, he will guide you into all truth: for he shall not speak of himself; but whatever he shall hear, that shall he speak: and he will show you things to come." John 16:13.

The Overcomes…" And they, (The believers), overcame him, (The devil), by the blood of the Lamb, and by the word of their testimony; and they loved not their lives unto the death." Revelation 12:12.

The Victory…" Be sober, be vigilant; because your adversary the devil, as a roaring lion, walks about, seeking whom he may devour. Resist him, standing firm in the faith, because you know that the family of believers throughout the world is undergoing the same kind of suffering." I Peter 5:8-9

So, **the origin of evil** **is** Lucifer, that wicked angel who rebelled against God and led 1/3 of all the "Heavenly Host" in a battle against God that ended with all of them being cast out of heaven.

The nature of evil is sin that manifests itself in wickedness, adultery, fornication, uncleanness, lasciviousness, idolatry, witchcraft, hatred, variance, emulations, wrath, strife, seditions, heresies, envying, murders, drunkenness, revellings, and much more. It is certainly unholy, unrighteous, and immoral. This is the nature of the Anti-Christ.

The destiny of evil *is* total eradication from the face of the earth. The personification of evil in all its forms, whether human or spirit, will be placed in the lake of fire for all eternity.

You may be thinking, "If evil is defeated, why are we Christians in a life-and-death battle with it? The answer is simple…because the devil has no power except that which we give him. He steals it from us with lies and suggestions that appeal to our evil nature. Multiply this by billions of men, women, boys, and girls and you amass lots of power. The devil takes all that power and rules through his captives. The battle is over, but the fight continues. God wants us to take dominion and rule over his enemies until he returns to earth.

Hear the words of Jesus on this wise…

"When the Son of man shall come in his glory, and all the holy angels with him, then shall he sit upon the throne of his glory: And before him shall be gathered all nations: and he shall separate them one from another, as a shepherd divides *his* sheep from the goats: And he shall set the sheep on his right hand, but the goats on the left. Then the King will say to those on his right, "Come, you who are blessed of my Father, inherit the kingdom prepared for you from the foundation of the world." Then shall he say also unto them on the left hand, "Depart from me, ye cursed, into everlasting fire, prepared for the devil and his angels:" Matthew 25:31-34 & 41.

Are you a sheep or are you a goat? Your destiny depends on your decision. It's time to decide. Being a sheep is to accept Jesus as Lord and Savior and allow him the privilege of sitting on the throne of your life. That involves repenting of your sins, getting off the throne of your life, and allowing Jesus his rightful place as your shepherd. Do it today and you will be "Born Again" into the family of God.

Living in the reality of God is easier when you know the devil's tricks and what he has in his toolbox.

The Devil's Toolbox

The devil, otherwise known as Satan, Beelzebub, The Evil One, The Thief, The Prince of Darkness, the Serpent and many other names has a "Toolbox" full of tricks and devices that he uses against human beings and especially the children of God. Most folks are unaware of the "Wiles" of the devil. Over 40% of Americans do not even believe that there is an actual devil, only that he is a symbol of evil. (Pew Report)

The Bible tells us about his tricks. His purpose is to snare us with one or more of his tools thereby creating a "Stronghold" in our lives, from which he can lord over us.

The literal meaning of a "Stronghold" is a fortified armed encampment that can be protected.

A "Snare" is a device or trap that is used to capture prey. It can be a hunter's trap for small game or a net that is used to catch fish in the sea.

The purpose of tricks, snares, and other tools in "The Devil's Toolbox" is to capture you, and dominate your thoughts and actions with the ultimate goal of manifesting his evil character through you. Hear what Jesus said about the thief, as he referred to the devil.

"The thief cometh not, but for to steal, and to kill, and to destroy: I am come that they might have life, and that they might have it more abundantly." John 10:10

Whatever you call this, "Evil Being" you must know, without a shadow of a doubt, that he is real, and he is after you to steal your dreams, kill any hope of happiness and destroy everything that is good in your life. He wants you dead, but not before he torments you for a lifetime.

News Flash

The good news is that Jesus has defeated the devil, and he has no power over you but what you give him. That is right, he must get you to use your own "Free Will" to accept his lies. That is how he takes control. Let us see what the scriptures say, so you know I am not making this up.

"And having spoiled principalities and powers, he (Jesus) made a shew of them openly, triumphing over them in it." Colossians 2:5

Jesus spoiled all evil principalities and powers. That is a total defeat. Then he made an open shew…this denotes an old Roman picture of conquest over enemies. The evil king and leaders were tied by a rope to the back of a chariot and led down the middle of the city streets in a procession of conquest so everyone could see and laugh at the defeated foe. This is a total victory.

The devil did not force Adam and Eve to submit when he tempted them in the Garden of Eden. They had to engage their "Free Will" to do what was suggested. Take a read:

There's Always Choices

"Now the serpent was more subtle than any beast of the field, which the LORD God had made. And he said unto the woman, Yea, hath God said, Ye shall not eat of every tree of the garden? But of the fruit of the tree which is in the midst of the garden, God hath said, Ye shall not eat of it, neither shall ye touch it, lest ye die.

And the serpent said unto the woman, Ye shall not surely die: For God doth know that in the day ye eat thereof, then your eyes shall be opened, and ye shall be as gods, knowing good and evil. And when the woman saw that the tree was good for food, and that it was pleasant to the eyes, and a tree to be desired to make one wise, she took of the fruit thereof, and did eat, and gave also unto her husband with her; and he did eat." Genesis 3:1-5.

The serpent is another name for the devil. He challenged the Word of God and persuaded Adam and Eve to believe that God was a liar, when in fact the liar was the devil. However, it was the "Free Will" of Adam and Eve that chose to believe the devil and disobey God.

More of The Devil's Toolbox

We have already seen one tool that is in the devil's toolbox. It is, "The Lie" Jesus, speaking to some religious leaders of his day, said this…

"Ye are of your father the devil, and the lusts of your father ye will do. He was a murderer from the beginning, and abode not in the truth, because there is no truth in him. When he speaks a lie, he speaks of his own: for he is a liar, and the father of it." John 8"44.

Lies That Kill, Steal & Destroy

How many times have we believed a lie? The politicians promise all kinds of things but never deliver. Are they lying? We believe their lies and then what?

Here are a few lies the devil uses to cause us to do what he wants.

Drugs cannot really hurt you. Try some and see for yourself.

Smoking is not really addictive.

Sex before marriage does not really hurt anyone.

Lying is acceptable as long as it doesn't harm anyone.

Taking a pen from work is not really stealing.

Drinking alcohol is cool.

Now let us look at some other lies that are active in modern societies

Ideology That Contradicts Bible Truth

The way you think is the basis for how you act and the way you live your life. There are certain lies that seek to alter your thought process, thereby changing your viewpoint. Here are a few:

There Is Only One True Church.

All the others are false. You must belong to our church to be saved. We are the true church of God.

This ideology is so untrue. Salvation does not come because of a church membership. Nor does it come from a, "True Religion" It comes from the finished work of Jesus Christ on the cross. He paid the price of sin with his own blood (death.) Hear what the scriptures say…

"Much more then, having now been justified by his blood, we shall be saved from the wrath of God through him. For if while we were enemies we were reconciled to God through the death of his Son, much more, having been reconciled, we shall be saved by his life. And not only this, but we also exult in God through our Lord Jesus Christ, through whom we have now received the reconciliation." Romans 5:9-11.

You Don't Have To Believe In Jesus To Attain Eternal Life.

The truth is, you do have to believe in Jesus, God's only begotten Son, to be saved and will not see heaven unless you accept him as Savior and Lord. (John 3:16) Hear what was said to the people of Israel.

"Be it known unto you all, and to all the people of Israel, that by the name of Jesus Christ of Nazareth, whom ye crucified, whom God raised from the dead, even by him doth this man stands here before you whole. This is the stone, which was set at naught of you builders, which is become the head of the corner. Neither is there salvation in any other: for there is none other name under heaven given among men, whereby we must be saved." Acts 4:10-12

I know what you might be thinking. What about those that have never heard about Jesus or do not understand? Do they go to hell? Here is an explanation I found from gotquestions.com. They are held accountable by the revelation of God in creation.

"For when the Gentiles, which have not the law, do by nature the things contained in the law, these, having not the law, are a law unto themselves: Which shew the work of the law written in their hearts, their conscience also bearing witness, and their thoughts the meanwhile accusing or else excusing one another" Romans 2:14-15

For the invisible things of him from the creation of the world are clearly seen, being understood by the things that are made, even his eternal power and Godhead; so that they are without excuse: Romans 1:20

It is foolish to debate the fairness of God sending someone to hell who never had the opportunity to hear the gospel of Christ. People are responsible to God for what God has already revealed to them through his creation. The Bible says that people reject this knowledge, and therefore God is just in condemning them to hell.

If we assume that those who never hear the gospel are granted mercy from God, we run into a terrible problem. If people who never hear the gospel are automatically saved, then it is logical to make sure no one ever hears the gospel—because then there would be a chance, they will reject it and be condemned. (*There is no "Get Out of Jail Free Cards*)

Listen to what the apostle John said: In the beginning was the Word and the Word was with God and the Word was God. The same was in the beginning with God. *All things were made by him, and without him was not anything made that was made." John 1:1-3* The Word that was God and is still God. He made everything. John goes on to say, And the Word (That pre-existed in heaven) was made flesh and dwelt among us (*And we beheld his glory as the only begotten Son of the Father), full of grace and truth"* John 1:14.

Now look at John 3:16. This is what Jesus said to Nicodemus, the religious ruler in Israel, "For **God so loved the world, that he gave his only begotten Son, that whosoever believeth in him should not perish, but have everlasting life.**"

It could not be clearer, to me anyway, that Jesus was and is the Word made flesh, sent by God the Father to save humanity. He is the *only begotten Son*, and it was he that created all things in the beginning…and it is he that men reject when they ignore the divine revelation of God in creation.

So, those who never heard of Jesus have already rejected the Son of God, their creator, and are accountable to him. (But, as it is written, they shall see, to whom no tidings of him came, and they who have not heard shall understand.) Romans 15:21 This is because God has revealed himself to every soul and even though they have not heard of Jesus, they have seen him in creation and understand who he is. If they seek to know, they will be led to a saving knowledge of Christ. If not, they will face him in final judgment. We will discuss this more in later chapters.

We Are All Children of God

Listen again to the scriptures. They reveal the truth.

"For as many as are led by the Spirit of God, they are the sons of God. For ye have not received the spirit of bondage again to fear; but ye have received the Spirit of adoption, whereby we cry, Abba, Father. The Spirit itself bears witness with our spirit, that we are the children of God**:**" Romans 8:14

If I Try To Be Good, That's Enough, Right?

The Bible tells us that even religious leaders will not see God's kingdom unless they are "Born Again" We must be "Born Again" to see God's kingdom. That is what Jesus said. Keep reading for the proof text.

"There was a man of the Pharisees, named Nicodemus, a ruler of the Jews: The same came to Jesus by night, and said unto him, Rabbi, we know that thou art a teacher come from God: for no man can do these miracles that thou do, except God be with him. Jesus answered and said unto him, Verily, verily, I say unto thee, except a man be born again, he cannot see the kingdom of God." John 3:3

There Are Many Ways To Heaven.

The lie is that we are all climbing the same mountain but by different paths. In other words, there are many ways to attain eternal life. This is in direct contrast to what Jesus said.

Listen…

"Enter ye in at the strait gate: for wide is the gate, and broad is the way, that leadeth to destruction, and many there be which go in thereat:" Matthew 7:13

The narrow gate is Jesus. He said himself that…well, read it for yourself…

"Let not your heart be troubled: ye believe in God, believe also in me. In my Father's house are many mansions: if it were not so, I would have told you. I go to prepare a place for you. And if I go and prepare a place for you, I will come again, and receive you unto myself; that where I am, there ye may be also. And whither I go ye know, and the way ye know. Thomas saith unto him, Lord, we know not whither thou goest; and how can we know the way? Jesus saith unto him, *I am the way, the truth, and the life*: *no man cometh unto the Father, but by me."* John 14:6

False Religions That Teach Heresy

How often have you heard someone say? "It does not matter what religion you follow. You will still end up in heaven." This lie extends into multiculturalism as well. People say it does not matter if you are Hindu, Muslim, Sikh, Buddhist, Catholic–whatever. It's not a religion that saves us, but a relationship with Jesus Christ.

There are many false religions in this world. I call some of them "Isms." They teach heresy and lead people astray. They distort the truth, deny the deity of Christ, and create a bondage that is very hard to break. Here are a few "Isms" to stay clear of. These are anti-Christ.

Relativism – Relativism is the idea that there is no such thing as truth. The devil does not want you to believe in truth because if there is no truth, then there is also no right and wrong, and if there is no right and wrong, then anything goes. He can tempt you into sin much more easily if he can first get you to believe there is no such thing as sin. Relativism is everywhere in our society. It takes many different forms.

Under Relativism, I can do my own thing. I can ignore any truth that does not line up with what I think. I am right all the time because there is no right or wrong, just whatever I want. This makes me my own god. How sad!

Utilitarianism – In Short…universalism is a theological doctrine that all human beings will eventually be saved: the principles and practices of a liberal Christian denomination founded in the 18th century originally to uphold the belief in "universal" salvation is now united with Unitarianism.

Here is the melting pot of all kinds of beliefs. You can believe anything you want and still be a member of this church because there is no standard or rule of practice, only what you think is right. The problem is… what we think is right is often wrong and with the devil lying to us; we can be easily misled unless we know God's truth. Jesus said… "Take heed therefore that the light which is in thee be not darkness." Luke 11:35

Jesus knew that much of what was being presented as truth or light was not truth at all. It was darkness. We need to stay away from such as this.

Atheism - Atheism is defined as the disbelief or lack of belief in the existence of God. Whereas, Theism is the belief in the existence of a God, especially belief in one God as creator of the universe, intervening in it and sustaining a personal relation to his creatures.

This non-religion premise has in modern times, become a religion unto itself. It denies God any place and sets man up as his own god. The end of this can only be eternal death.

"There is a way which seems right unto a man, but the end thereof are the ways of death." Proverbs 14:12.

Mormonism - The Mormon religion, (Mormonism), whose followers are known as Mormons and Latter-Day Saints (LDS), was founded less than two hundred years ago by a man named Joseph Smith. He claimed to have received a personal visit from God the Father and Jesus Christ who told him that all churches and their creeds were an abomination. Joseph Smith then set out to begin a brand-new religion that claims to be the "only true church on earth.

This doctrine is a lie and a distortion of the truth. It is a humanistic approach to religion that denies the deity of Christ, the God Head, The Gifts of the Spirit, and many other Bible norms.

Socialism - By the late 19th century, socialism emerged as "the most influential secular movement of the twentieth century, worldwide. It is a political ideology (or world view), a wide and divided political movement" Socialist parties and ideas remain a political force with varying degrees of power and influence on all continents, heading national governments in many countries around the world.

Today, some socialists have also adopted the causes of other social movements, such as environmentalism, feminism, and progressivism. They reject religion, and faith and are anti-God

Satanism - is a group of ideological and philosophical beliefs based on Satan. Contemporary religious practice of Satanism began with the founding of the Church of Satan in 1966, although a few historical precedents exist.

Prior to the public practice, Satanism existed primarily as an accusation by various Christian groups toward perceived ideological opponents, rather than a self-identity. Satanism, and the concept of Satan, has also been used by artists and entertainers for symbolic expression.

Liberalism - Unlike traditional liberalism, there is a certain element of tyranny within the modern liberal movement. In past centuries, liberalism was used to literally liberate people from the rule of kings and tyrants.

Modern liberalism is now imposing its immoral beliefs onto people who are not interested in focusing their lives around how their state can help them; it is a forced movement that is functioning more like a tyranny than any other liberal beliefs have ever done. The premise of liberalism is mainly centered in anti-conservativism which rejects moral laws and respect for tradition.

The devil pushes liberalism more on the young, encouraging immoral behavior or anything that is anti-God.

Legalism... (or nomism), in Messianic Christian theology, is the act of putting the Law of Moses above the gospel, which is 1 Corinthians 15:1-4, by establishing requirements for salvation beyond faith (trust) in Jesus Christ, specifically, trust in his finished work - the shedding of his blood for our sins, and reducing the broad, inclusive, and general precepts of the Bible to narrow and rigid moral codes.

It is an over-emphasis of discipline of conduct, or legal ideas, usually implying an allegation of misguided rigor, pride, superficiality, the neglect of mercy, and ignorance of the grace of God or emphasizing the letter of law at the expense of the spirit.

Here are a few non "isms" but equally as anti-God:

Witchcraft – This is the practice of magic or sorcery by anyone outside the religious mainstream of a society. This term is used in different ways in different times and places. Witchcraft is part of the Occult that denies God and rejects Jesus as Lord. It is centered in mysticism and preys on uniformed folks that seek spiritual answers.

Jehovah's Witness - The Jehovah's Witnesses are best known for going door-to-door. You have probably seen them in your area, and more than likely they have knocked on your door. They recently spent over 1.2 billion hours in one year proclaiming the so-called "good news of Jehovah and his kingdom".

Jehovah's Witnesses reject the Trinity, believing Jesus to be a created being and the Holy Spirit to essentially be the inanimate power of God. Jehovah's Witnesses reject the concept of Christ's substitutionary atonement and instead hold to a ransom theory, that Jesus' death was a ransom payment for Adam's sin.

New Age - The **New Age** is a term applied to a range of spiritual or religious beliefs and practices that developed in Western nations during the 1970s. Precise scholarly definitions of the movement differ in their emphasis, largely because of its highly eclectic structure. Although analytically often considered to be religious, those involved in it typically prefer the designation of "spiritual" and rarely use the term "New Age" themselves. Many scholars of the subject refer to it as the *New Age movement*. It is very close to Universalism in that it believes in the spiritual but denied the truth of One God, One Lord, and One Spirit, which is the centerpiece of Christianity.

Islam - "The source of the word, (Allah), who is the Islamic god, goes back to pre- Muslim times. Islam calls Allah god, which is not the God of the bible. Allah has about 1.6 billion followers worldwide. In 2010, Muslims made up 23.2% of the global population. According to the Encyclopedia of Religion, Allah corresponded to the Babylonian god Baal, and Arabs knew of him long before Mohammed worshipped him as the supreme god.

Before Islam, the Arabs recognized many gods and goddesses; each tribe had their own deity. There were also nature deities. Allah was the god of the local Quraish tribe, which was Mohammed's tribe before he invented Islam to lead his people out of their polytheism. Allah was then known as the Moon god, who had three daughters who were viewed as intercessors for the people.

Demonic Suggestions

We could go on and on but you get the point, right? There is a suggestion made by the devil to us that is a lie. It is presented as truth. If we believe it, we fall prey to the devil's manipulation and he eventually takes over. He wants to be the "Voice in Your Head" that lords over you. He wants to lead you away from all that is Godly.

All that has been mentioned above deal with lies that if accepted and believed will capture you and lead you from the light of God's glory into darkness.

Pitfalls In Personality…The Deeds of The Flesh

Now here are a few inward traps that cause sickness in our bodies and hasten our demise. These character flaws are used by the devil to capture us and take us down the road to destruction. They are a product of our own fallen nature. The Bible calls them the "Works of The Flesh." There is a full list in Galatians 5:19-21

"Now the works of the flesh are manifest, which are these; adultery, fornication, uncleanness, lasciviousness, idolatry, witchcraft, hatred, variance, emulations, wrath, strife, seditions, heresies, envyings, murders, drunkenness, revellings, and such like: of the which I tell you before, as I have also told you in time past, that they which do such things shall not inherit the kingdom of God." Galatians 5:19-21

All the devil needs to do is to suggest a plan of action that involves one or more of these character flaws and if you buy it, you're off into the flesh that cannot please God. If he tells you that your brother's wife is sexy and you probably could have her and you start thinking of the reality of that encounter, you have committed adultery. Lust takes over, ego soars and your imagination rules. You do not have to do the act, just think about it.

The same is true of "Pornography." If you are just looking, it is still fornication in your mind and that will distort your sense of morality and steal your Godly values. "But I say unto you, that whosoever looks on a woman to lust after her hath committed adultery with her already in his heart." Matthew 5:28

The devil does not make you do it. He only suggests that you do it. It is your own will that takes you down the road to hell.

Accusations That Destroy Self-Confidence

The Bible says that Satan, (the devil) is the accuser of the brethren. Here is the exact scripture…

"And I heard a loud voice saying in heaven, Now is come salvation, and strength, and the kingdom of our God, and the power of his Christ: for the accuser of our brethren is cast down, which accused them before our God Day and night. And they overcame him by the blood of the Lamb, and by the word of their testimony; and they loved not their lives unto the death." Revelation 12:10-11

The, "They" in Verse 11 is us, "The Brethren." We can and do overcome this accuser with "The Blood of The Lamb, The Word of Our Testimony and Because We Loved Not Our Lives Unto Death". …we can have victory.

You may be wondering what types of accusations are made against us. Here are a few:

- You are ugly and stupid.
- You are not worthy of anyone's love.
- You cannot be saved because you have done too many bad things.
- You are a bad person so go ahead and be bad.
- You are too fat.

- You will never amount to anything.
- And so on.

Demonic accusations are meant to cause doubt, fear, low self-esteem and worry among other things. However, the scripture (12:11) also says that the accusation is against you is being made before the throne of God. He accuses you in front of all the host of heaven. All the things you do wrong are brought before the court of God's justice. He is constantly telling God what you have done wrong. If we are "Born Again" Jesus, who is seated at the right hand of God, The Father, is interceding on our behalf, said in effect, "He or she is mine. Their names are written in the Lamb's Book of Life. They have been washed in my Blood."

Demonic Strategies That Attack Right Thinking

Larry R. Lawrence offers these four demonic strategies that the devil uses to defeat God's children. We need to know what they are and look for them in our daily experiences so we can stop them from hurting us.

Temptation… Satan pushes us to act on addictive urges and to entertain selfishness and greed. How can we resist this direct temptation? Jesus used a two-step defensive technique: first, he ordered Satan to leave; then he quoted scripture. You have the right to tell Satan to leave when you are confronted with temptation. There is great power in memorizing scripture, as Jesus did. Scripture power not only intimidates Satan, but it also brings the Spirit of God into your heart. Listen again to the scriptures.

"There hath no temptation taken you but such as is common to man: but God is faithful, who will not suffer you to be tempted above that ye are able; but will with the temptation also make a way to escape, that ye may be able to bear it". I Corinthians, chapter 10.

Deception… The devil has been called "the great deceiver." He attempts to counterfeit every true principle that the Lord presents. Although Satan will lie to you, you can count on the Spirit of God to tell you the truth. That is why the gift of the Holy Ghost is so essential.

The devil will try to deceive you at every turn in life. He will try to get you to believe that right is wrong and wrong is right. Immorality is not wrong. It is just different. Abortion is not wrong. It is just a women's health issue. See how it works?

Contention… Satan is the father of contention. He delights in seeing good people argue. When there is contention in your home or workplace, immediately stop whatever you are doing and seek to make peace. It does not matter who started it.

"Be not hasty in thy spirit to be angry: for anger rests in the bosom of fools." Ecclesiastes 7:9

We do not want to be counted with the fools of this world. However, the devil wants us there so he and the rest of the inhabitants of planet earth can laugh at us.

Discouragement… Satan effectively uses this tool on the most faithful Saints when all else fails. President Ezra Taft Benson (1899–1994) gave suggestions for fighting discouragement. They include serving others; working hard and avoiding idleness; practicing good health habits; seeking a priesthood blessing; listening to inspiring music; counting your blessings; and setting goals. Above all, as the scriptures teach, we are to pray always so we can conquer Satan.

When we get discouraged, it is usually because we did not get our way. Something hindered us from being on top. Instead, we got fired, do not win in a card game, watched as our spouse left us, or some other bad thing.

There is an easy remedy for discouragement. That is to make Jesus the Lord of your life and trust him in every circumstance. This takes the burden of responsibility off you and allows God to work out everything for good.

Materialism That Denies the Hereafter

I am not talking about going to the mall to shop until you drop. That is a minor form of materialism. The deeper problem is the growing conviction that there is no supernatural realm. God, the angels, demons, heaven, and hell are just a myth. There is no invisible world.

The church is just an institution of man's making by which he controls the masses. The pastors, priests, and church leaders are no more than social workers. Marriage is just a piece of paper, and salvation is unnecessary because there is no afterlife. That is materialism. Do you recognize it?

It is anti-God in every way because it rejects any future existence after death. The irony is that this type of thinking makes life a total waste. The fact that we exist has no meaning. If we become rich and powerful or just live life normally makes no difference. Whatever we do is without purpose because it really does not matter because there is no afterlife, judgment, or reward. We need to resist this type of reasoning at all costs. It is a lie. God does exist. There is an afterlife. We will be held accountable for our actions.

Situational Ethics That Replaces Absolute Truth

This is another name for moral relativism. The idea is that nothing is right or wrong except for the intentions and circumstances of the moral choice. If you mean well and the circumstances justify it, then what you have chosen to do is okay. Huge numbers of Christians have accepted this premise to justify abortion. If it feels right, it must be ok. However, feeling right is not the same as God's moral laws. His "Word" is absolute, no matter what you or I feel.

The devil will always invoke a situational ethic into the mix to divert our thinking away from the absolute truth of God's Word. Here is an example of situational sin…

We all know that it is wrong to steal. It is so stated in the 10-Commandments that man shall not steal. However, if I am hungry and have no money and am down on my luck, it is ok to swipe a loaf of bread from a supermarket or a candy bar from a drugstore. Right? Wrong! Wrong! Wrong! The situation does not override God's law. It is always wrong to steal, no matter the reason for which we do it.

Scientific Facts That Contradict Biblical Revelation

This is the idea that the only truth is scientific truth. It is a powerful lie of Satan because it is one of those things, which is simply assumed in society.

"We all know that science has disproved the Bible, right?" Wrong. All truth is God's truth and true science is always the sister of true theology. Scientism is an offshoot of atheism. "There is no God. There are just the laws of science. That is all." No! No! No! That type of thinking is wrong.

This Godless doctrine ushered in evolution back in the 18th century. It was the devil's way of offering a believable platform for those who did not want to follow God. As you may know, this theory says we evolved over millions of years into what we are today, with no divine influence. Thus, we are our own gods and masters of our own destinies. Hitler used this theory to kill six million Jews in WWII. African Americans were once considered sub- standard beings because of this theory. Hear what the Bible says…

"And as it is appointed unto men once to die, but after this the judgment: So Christ was once offered to bear the sins of many; and unto them that look for him shall he appear the second time without sin unto salvation." Hebrews 9:27-28 We should look to Jesus, not science.

A "Snare" or Trap That Captures the Unaware

The devil will use anything he can to capture us and use us to do his will. It can be hatred, jealousy, pride, sex, gluttony, fame, fortune, power, and the like. All he has to do is set the trap, dangle the bait in front of us and wait for us to engage our free will to go after it. Christians, "Beware!"

False Prophets & Teachers That Lead People Astray

Here is what the Bible says about false prophets and teachers…

"And many false prophets shall rise, and shall deceive many." Matthew 24:11 Mark 13:22 said it this way…" For false Christs and false prophets shall rise, and shall shew signs and wonders, to seduce, if it were possible, even the elect."

The goal of these false prophets is to deceive. Their teachings are false. Their efforts are for self-empowerment. Their doctrines are demonic. Have you ever heard of Rev. Jones that took his congregation overseas and killed them all… but only after abusing the females and stealing their wealth?

Let us bring this on the level of the average Christian who can also be a false teacher. Here again what Jesus said to his disciples:

"For many shall come in my name, saying, I am Christ; and shall deceive many.: Matthew 24:5 The term, "Christ" literally means anointed. What is really being said is that there will be many that claim to be anointed of God, like Jesus was anointed. This is the mark of a Christian but these false Christians are not anointed. They just claim to be. They will be able to talk the talk but do not follow the truth of the gospel message.

A good example is the Mormon Church. These days they claim to be the Latter-Day Saints and call themselves Christians. However, they believe very differently. Their doctrines are anti-Christ. These false believers are sprinkled throughout all mainline denominations.

How many folks do you know that profess to be a Christian but have no knowledge of what it really means? Some even claim to be anointed when they operate in the flesh and promote a secular gospel, that is akin to humanism.

Sickness & Disease That Kills the Body

The devil will use sickness and disease to steal our strength, destroy our health and kill our healthy cells. However, we are challenged to believe another report. This time it's not the doctor's diagnosis but the "Divine Healer's Report."

The question is, "Does God Want You To Be Healed or Will he Say No To Your Plea?" I was uniformed, way back when. My prayer for healing always started with, "If It Be Thy Will" I never knew if it was God's will to heal or not. Maybe there was a reason he didn't want us to be healed. Then I looked into the scriptures and found these declarations:

Healed By His Stripes

"He is despised and rejected of men; a man of sorrows, and acquainted with grief: and we hid as it were our faces from him; he was despised, and we esteemed him not. Surely, he hath borne our griefs, and carried our sorrows: yet we did esteem him stricken, smitten of God, and afflicted. But he was wounded for our transgressions, he was bruised for our iniquities: the chastisement of our peace was upon him; *and with his stripes we are healed.*" Isaiah 5.:3-6 "Who hath believed our report? and to whom is the arm of the LORD revealed?" Isaiah 53:1.

Note: This suffering servant, spoken of by Isaiah, has borne our grief and carried our sorrows. He was stricken of God. He was wounded for our transgressions and bruised for our iniquities. The chastisement of our peace was upon him….and "With His Stripes, We Are Healed."

The only person that qualifies in all these areas is Jesus. Isaiah clearly said that our healing is in his stripes, which were his beatings and bruises and wounds. His blood and subsequent death brought healing to those who believed his report.

Expectations That Discourage "Free Will" Choices

The devil often uses people to do his bidding. It could be a parent, co-worker, teacher or even a friend. Their efforts to impose expectations on you can be very painful. It could be an immoral act, a restrictive influence or even a command that goes against what you feel is right.

This type of expectation puts pressure on you to be or do what they want instead of what you feel is right. It is a form of oppression.

On the other hand, God's expectations are designed to give you the greatest freedom and blessings possible. Hear what the psalmist said many years ago, "my soul, wait thou only upon God; for my expectation is from him." Psalm 62:5

If you feel that what others are expecting of you is not in God's plan for your life or that you just do not have peace about what is expected of you, reject it, no matter who it is. Your peace is more important than their expectations. That will keep the devil at bay and you free. We should always look for what God would expect of us and reject the expectations of others. By the way, God's expectations are clearly revealed in the Bible.

Illusions & Mind Games That Confuse And Manipulate

The devil will also use illusions to confuse you or cause you to think that he has power over you or cause you to think that he owns the world and even people in it. Listen to how he tried to trick Jesus…

"The devil said to him, (Jesus), "I will give you all the power and glory of these kingdoms. All of it has been given to me, and I give it to anyone I please." Luke 4:6.

The devil did not own the kingdoms of the world. Nor did he have the power and glory of those kingdoms. They belong to God. "The earth is the LORD's, and the fullness thereof; the world, and they that dwell therein. For he hath founded it upon the seas and established it upon the floods." Psalm 24:1-2.

As the story goes, the devil took Jesus up to the pinnacle of the temple to show him all the kingdoms of the world. The problem is, you cannot see all the kingdoms of the world from that vantage point.

The devil likes to play with your mind and manipulate your imagination. He will play mind games with you in hopes that you will engage your imagination to mentally see what is being suggested. It all takes place in the mind and it is usually a bold-faced lie.

Here is how it works with folks today. A thought enters the mind of a kid that is from the devil or one of his demons. He is in a store looking at a toy truck. The suggestion is, "Take it, no one is looking. The kid mentally sees himself playing with it and sees all his friends being envious of him because he has a new truck and they do not… so he steals it.

It could be a lonely guy wishing he could find a girl. Suddenly, a thought enters his mind. It is of an old girlfriend. Another thought tells him, "Boy, I could really …*you can fill in the rest*. Now he is mentally engaged in a sexual act that is not real…thus, he falls into sin, gets depressed because he realizes he is still alone, hates himself for thinking that way and becomes suicidal.

The devil will always suggest that you picture things that you do not or cannot have. He does this because it is tormenting and he loves to torment us as he takes us down the road to hell. His goal is to drive you to a place where you will act out your fantasies. Thus, comes rape, murder, watching pornography and all the deeds of the flesh listed in Galatians chapter five.

The thing to realize is…*not all our thoughts are ours*. We get some from the devil, from our own sinful nature, and even some from the Holy Spirit. We must try the spirits to be sure they are from God before we act on them. Hear what the apostle John says…

"Beloved, believe not every spirit, but try the spirits whether they are of God: because many false prophets are gone out into the world. Hereby know ye the Spirit of God: Every spirit that confesses that Jesus Christ is come in the flesh is of God: And every spirit that confesses not that Jesus Christ is come in the flesh is not of God: and this is that spirit of antichrist, whereof ye have heard that it should come; and even now already is it in the world." I John 4:1-5

Jesus used the scriptures to defeat the devil. He said, ***"IT IS WRITTEN."*** He knew the Word of God and used it to put down the lie and dispel the illusion. This means if we want to defeat the devil, we also need to know what is written so we can use it at the appropriate time. I am referring to the written Word of God, the Bible. If we are tempted to steal, we can say to ourselves," it is written." Then we can quote scripture as did Jesus, "Thou Shalt Not Steal" Exodus 20:15 This will dispel the illusion. Then we can tell the devil to take a hike.

Knowing scripture is essential to winning the battle. Here is what Paul said to the Corinthian church back in the first century, "For the weapons of our warfare are not carnal but mighty in God for pulling down strongholds, casting down imaginations and every high thing that exalts itself above the knowledge of God, bringing every thought into captivity to the obedience of Christ" II Corinthians 10:4-5

If we know the scripture, we can cast down every imagination that is against the knowledge of God. That is what Jesus did. He knew that God said that man was not to steal, and he used that truth to overcome the devil.

Remember, what God did in the Old Testament was then. We are now in a New Covenant where God's grace (Un-Merited Favor) rules the day. God does not punish his children with disease or sickness. His loving hand is extended towards all who believe. He wants them all to come to repentance.

I am sure you will find other tools that should be added to the devil's toolbox. I have shown you enough to open your eyes to the "Wiles" of the devil in hopes that you search out ways to defend yourself. We are in a fight for our lives that has eternal consequences.

The apostle Peter gave us a clear and present danger with an assurance of victory. Here's what he said,

"Be sober, be vigilant; because your adversary the devil, as a roaring lion, walketh about, seeking whom he may devour: Whom resist steadfast in the faith, knowing that the same afflictions are accomplished in your brethren that are in the world." I Peter 5:8-9.

The apostle Paul said this about that, "For the weapons of our warfare are not carnal, but mighty through God to the pulling down of strongholds;) Casting down imaginations, and every high thing that exalts itself against the knowledge of God, and bringing into captivity every thought to the obedience of Christ "2 Corinthians 10:4-5:

The apostle John leaves us with this…" And now, little children, abide in him; that, when he shall appear, we may have confidence, and not be ashamed before him at his coming." I John 2:28.

Knowing all these things helps us to attain and enjoy the reality of God. This is our destiny, our life's ambition, and our ultimate goal.

CHAPTER SIX:
"HOW TO" ESCAPE THE REALITY OF HELL

Attaining and enjoying the reality of God can only be accomplished if we face the reality of hell and be sure we are not going there.

This teaching is written to expose the myth that hell does not exist and that there is no judgment or eternal punishment. We will also learn how to escape the damnation that will fall upon the children of disobedience.

The end of days is fast approaching and we need to be assured of our salvation and focused on those things that really count. Knowing that there is a hell and understanding how to escape it, as a destiny, is the most important thing anyone can do.

How many times have you told someone to, **"Go To Hell"?** How many times has someone told you the same thing? If we knew the type of place that hell is, we would not be telling others to go there.

Webster defines hell as "A place regarded in various religions as a spiritual realm of evil and suffering, often traditionally depicted as a place of perpetual fire beneath the earth where the wicked are punished after death."

The Bible definition goes like this, "Hell" is the future place of eternal punishment of the damned including the devil and his fallen angels. There are several words rendered as "Hell"

Hades--A Greek word. It is the place of the dead--the location of the person between death and resurrection. *(See Matt. 11:23, 16:18, Acts 11:27, 1 Cor.*

15:55, Rev. 1:18, 6:8).

Gehenna--A Greek word. It was the place where dead bodies were dumped and burned **(2 Kings 23:13-14)**. Jesus used the word to designate the place of eternal torment **(Matt. 5:22, 29, 30, Mark 9:43, Luke 12:5).**

Sheol--A Hebrew word. It is the place of the dead and not necessarily the grave but the place the dead go to. It is used of both the righteous **(Psalm 16:10, 30:3**, **Isaiah 38:10)** and the wicked **(Num. 16:33, Job. 24:19, Psalm 9:17).**

Hell… is a place of eternal fire **(Matt. 25:41, Rev. 19:20)**. It was prepared for the devil and his angels **(Matt. 25:41)** and will be the abode of the wicked **(Rev. 21:8)** and the fallen angels **(2 Pet. 2:4)**."

It's not a place where the average folks would want to go, visit or live. But, according to Jesus, many will go there. "Enter ye in at the strait gate: for wide *is* the gate, and broad *is* the way, that leads to destruction, and many there be which go in thereat:" Matthew 7:13

The Horror of Hell

Tom Ascol of Ligonier Ministries shares four truths about hell that Jesus taught in Matthew 25:41-46. These truths should cause us to grieve over the prospect of anyone experiencing its horrors.

First, **hell is a state of separation from God**. On the day of judgment, Jesus will said to all unbelievers, "Depart from me, you cursed, into the eternal fire" (v. 41). This is the same sort of language that Jesus uses elsewhere to describe the final judgment of unbelievers (see 7:23).

To be separated from God is to be separated from anything and everything good. That is hard to understand because even the most miserable person enjoys some of God's blessings. We breathe his air, are nourished by food that he supplies, and experience many other aspects of his common grace.

On earth, even atheists enjoy the benefits of God's goodness. But in hell, these blessings will be nonexistent. Those consigned there will remember God's goodness, and will even have some awareness of the unending pleasures of heaven, but they will have no access to them.

This does not mean that God will be completely absent from hell. He is and will remain omnipresent (Ps. 139:7–8). To be separated from the Lord and cast into hell does not mean that a person will finally be free of God. That person will remain eternally accountable to him. He will remain Lord over the person's existence. But in hell, a person will be forever separated from God in his kindness, mercy, grace, and goodness. He will be consigned to deal with him in his holy wrath.

Secondly, **hell is a state of association**. Jesus said that the eternal fire of hell was "prepared for the devil and his angels" (Matt. 25:41). People were made for God. Hell was made for the devil. Yet people who die in their sin, without Jesus Christ as Lord and Savior, will spend eternity in hell with the one being who is most unlike God. It is a tragic irony that many who do not believe in the devil in this life will wind up spending eternity being tormented with him in hell.

The third truth is that Hell is a state of punishment. Jesus describes it as "fire" (v. 41) and a place of "punishment" (v. 46). Hell is a place of retribution where justice is served through the payment for crimes.

The punishment must fit the crime. The misery and torment of hell points to the wickedness and seriousness of sin. Those who protest the Biblical doctrine of hell as being excessive betray their inadequate comprehension of the sinfulness of sin. For sinners to be consigned to anything less than the horrors of eternal punishment would be a miscarriage of justice.

Finally, the fourth truth is that hell is an everlasting state. Though some would like to shorten the duration of this state, Jesus' words are very clear. He uses the same adjective to describe both punishment and life in verse 46. If hell is not eternal, neither is the new heaven and earth.

How can God exact infinite punishment for a finite sin? First, because the person against whom all sin is committed is infinite. Crimes against the infinitely holy, infinitely kind, infinitely good, and infinitely supreme Ruler of the world deserve unending punishment. Besides that, those condemned to hell will go on sinning for eternity. There is no repentance in hell. So, the punishment will continue as long as the sinning does.

The dreadfulness of hell deepens our grateful praise for the salvation we have in Jesus Christ. Hell is what we deserve and hell is what he experienced on the cross in our place.

Believing the truth about hell also motivates us to persuade people to be reconciled to God. By God's grace, those of us who are trusting Christ have been rescued from this horrible destiny. How can we love people and refuse to speak plainly to them about the reality of eternal damnation and God's gracious provision of salvation? Clearer visions of hell will give us greater love for both God and people.

How Can A Loving God *Condemn So Many To Hell*

I have a few friends that tell me, in no uncertain terms, that they cannot understand how a loving God can damn to hell so many people. It is obvious that they do not comprehend the concept of the "Free Will" of man.

God is in full control of his creation. Part of that control is to allow man to have a free will to also be in full control. It's all a matter of sovereignty.

When you gather thousands or even a few folks together that are all exercising their free will, things can get ugly. Some will get drunk; others will kill or steal and yet others will exercise righteous judgment in life. All this interaction of free wills brings on different opinions, different lifestyles, and different attitudes.

If God intervenes to stop the flow of our "Free will" decisions, he tampers with the future and denies man his right to be a free moral agent. His actions would contradict his own will and plan for humanity. Man must be free to choose his own way to escape a robotic existence that is not what God or man wants.

However, with this gift of "Free Will" comes responsibility. The Bible says that the soul that sins will die…" Behold, all souls are mine; as the soul of the father, so also the soul of the son is mine: the soul that sins, it shall die." Ezekiel 18:4 ("Be not deceived; God is not mocked: for whatsoever a man soweth, that shall he also reap.") Galatians 6:7 ("For all have sinned, and come short of the glory of God;") Romans 3:23.

It should be obvious by now that **God sends no one to hell**. He does, however, allow mankind to send themselves to hell by their own choices in life. Our life choices do affect our destiny. They take us down the road to destruction or up the road to eternal life.

This concept is not new. We need only to look at a man that drinks a lot and we can conclude that if he does not slack off, he will become a drunk. We can see it coming. The same is true when we look at a person who cares not about their eternal soul, lives for today, denies the existence of God and ignores the truths of the Bible. We can say, if he does not repent, he will ultimately end up in hell. We can see it coming.

I have already delt with those that have never heard the gospel and what happens to them in chapter five.

Is The Devil In Charge of Hell?

No, the devil is not in charge of anything, but is thrown into hell and ultimately the lake of fire according to Revelation 20:10. There is no party in hell for the lost. There is no reward. There is no pleasure at all.

Where Is Hell?

Your guess is as good as mine. People have put forward various theories on the location of hell. A traditional view is that hell is in the center of the earth. Others propose that hell is located in outer space in a black hole. In the Old Testament, the word translated "hell" is Sheol; in the New Testament, it's Hades (meaning "unseen") and Gehenna ("the Valley of Hinnom"). Sheol is also translated as "pit" and "grave." Both Sheol and Hades refer to a temporary abode of the dead before judgment (Psalm 9:17; Revelation 1:18). Gehenna refers to an eternal state of punishment for the wicked dead (Mark 9:43).

In the King James Version, Ephesians 4:9 said that before Jesus ascended into heaven, "he also descended.. . into the lower parts of the earth." Some Christians take "the lower parts of the earth" as a reference to hell, where they said Jesus spent the time between his death and resurrection. However, the New International Version gives a better translation: "he also descended to the lower, earthly regions." This verse simply says that Jesus came to earth. It's a reference to his incarnation, not to his location after death.

The notion that hell is somewhere in outer space, possibly in a black hole, is based on the knowledge that black holes are places of great heat and pressure from which nothing, not even light, can escape. Surprisingly, this concept of hell is presented in the 1979 Walt Disney film The Black Hole.

Another speculation is that the earth itself will be the "lake of fire" spoken of in Revelation 20:10-15. When the earth is destroyed by fire (2 Peter 3:10; Revelation 21:1), as the theory goes, God will use that burning sphere as the everlasting place of torment for the ungodly. Again, this is mere speculation.

To sum up, Scripture does not tell us the geological (or cosmological) location of hell. Hell is a literal place of real torment, but we do not know where it is. Hell may have a physical location in this universe, or it may be in an entirely different "dimension." Whatever the case, the location of hell is far less important than the need to avoid going there.

What Is Hell Really Like?

The Bible tells us that God is light and that there is no darkness in him. When a soul is separated from God, there is no light, only total darkness. There are no friendships, only total isolation…all alone forever. It is a place of torment. I believe that the ultimate torment is to see God, feel his love and splendor and must live with the fact that you can never have it.

I also see the deep cravings of the flesh being manifested, but never fulfilled. Then there is the fire and stench of burning flesh. This type of fire cannot be quenched. It will burn with the wrath of God forever.

I realize that this is a morbid picture and a horrible destiny but that is what Jesus said, "There shall be weeping and gnashing of teeth, when ye shall see Abraham, and Isaac, and Jacob, and all the prophets, in the kingdom of God, and you yourselves thrust out". Luke 13:28.

The Controversy Over Eternal Suffering of The Wicked and Their Annihilation

There is a controversy over eternal suffering and annihilation. Some folks believe that the souls in hell suffer forever. Others read "And death and hell were cast into the lake of fire. This is the second death." Revelation 20:14 and conclude that this 2nd death is total annihilation.

The premise for this conclusion is, "And God shall wipe away all tears from their eyes; and there shall be no more death, neither sorrow, nor crying, neither shall there be any more pain: for the former things are passed away." Revelation 21:14.

The thought is that our tears are caused by knowing some of our loved ones are suffering in hell and the fact that we remember them no more is because of the end of their suffering by the 2nd death. As hopeful as this thought process is, it is not Biblical because it goes against what God has spoken about the wicked and their destiny.

Many folks that do not believe in God, said, "Even if there is a God and he sends me to hell, it's not forever". "I will end up non-existent, as though I never existed…so, that justifies my so-called sin now, to eat, drink and be merry." Without an absolute penalty, there is no fear of judgment because the punishment is temporary.

When God wipes away all our tears, I believe he removes the memory of all the bad stuff, including those that chose against God and ended up in eternal damnation.

Are People Suffering in Hell Right Now?

Jesus related a story about a rich man and a beggar. Here is what he said as recorded by Luke 16:20-24.

"And there was a certain beggar named Lazarus, which was laid at his gate, full of sores and desiring to be fed with the crumbs, which fell from the rich man's table: moreover, the dogs came and licked his sores.

And it came to pass, that the beggar died, and was carried by the angels into Abraham's bosom: the rich man also died, and was buried; **And in hell he lifted his eyes, being in torment** and sees Abraham afar off, and Lazarus in his bosom.

And he cried and said, Father Abraham, have mercy on me, and send Lazarus, that he may dip the tip of his finger in water, and cool my tongue; for I am tormented in this flame.

I realize that this was just a story that Jesus related. However, there are several important points to consider:

The wicked die and find themselves in hell in torment. It is an immediate happening. It is therefore a picture of reality. The Bible also confirms this, "And as it is appointed unto men once to die, but after this the judgment" Hebrews 9:27.

- The torment was hell fire.
- The suffering was of the body and soul.
- Those assigned to hell cannot leave.

- They have no way to quench the flames or find any sort of comfort.

They could hear, thirst, feel pain and sorrow, and even communicate with those in paradise. But the one thing that the people in hell could not do was to cease to exist.

After the resurrection of Christ, things concerning hell changed. Jesus went to hell, took the keys of hell and death (Rev. 1:18), and set the captives free—those who were in Abraham's bosom.

Ephesians 4: 9-10 says,

"Now that he ascended, what is it but that he also descended first into the lower parts of the earth? He that descended is the same also that ascended up far above all heavens, that he might fill all things."

After defeating the devil and setting the captives free, Jesus took those in Abraham's bosom to heaven with him, where all believers go now. But we will not live in heaven forever. We only live in heaven until the end of the age. Then God is going to make a new heaven and a new earth, and all the believers will live there with Jesus in the new Jerusalem which is on the new earth. (Rev. 21:1-4)

When you die in your sins, you go straight to hell. You do not pass go or collect $200. The game is over and you lost big-time. You experience death physically, torment until the end of all things and then a 2nd death of your eternal soul as it is cast into the lake of fire. Your suffering will last forever.

"And fear not them which kill the body, but are not able to kill the soul: but rather fear him which is able to destroy both soul and body in hell." Matthew 10:28

Although it was never intended for man, hell is an awful place where those who reject so great a sacrifice will join the devil and his angels for eternity. (Rev. 20:10)

The Unpardonable Sin

The Bible makes it clear that the Holy Spirit convicts us of sin, and there is only one sin that can send us to hell. That is the sin of rejecting the sacrifice of Jesus Christ.

"And when he (the Holy Spirit) is come, he will reprove the world of sin (singular), and of righteousness, and of judgment: of sin, because they believe not on me." (John 16: 8-) Excerpts taken from Andrew Womack Ministries article "Hell, A Reality or Metaphor?"

The Final Punishment of The Wicked

There is a punishment for sinners who refuse to repent. In Revelation 20:13-15 we read of a resurrection of the dead where people will be judged, "And whosoever was not found written in the book of life was cast into the lake of fire." (These are the folks that willingly rejected Jesus, God's only begotten Son, as the sacrifice for their sin.)

When you are "Born Again," your name is written in the "Book of Life." If you name is not there, you are counted with the wicked, no matter what good you may have done while alive.

Being a saint and being "Born Again" is not determined by what you do or don't do. It is determined by what Jesus did. He lived a perfect life in accordance to God's law and as the perfect Lamb of God, without blemish, became the sacrifice on the cross of Calvary, as the penalty for sin. This is the essence of the Gospel or Good News. Paul, the apostle, put it this way, "For by grace (Unmerited Favor) are ye saved through faith; and that not of yourselves: *it is* the gift of God:" Ephesians 2:8

As I mentioned previously, the punishment of the wicked dead in hell is described throughout scripture as "eternal fire" (Matthew 25:41), "unquenchable fire" (Matthew 3:12), "shame and everlasting contempt" (Daniel 12:2), a place where "the fire is not quenched" (Mark 9:44-49), a place of "torment" and "fire" (Luke 16:23-24), "everlasting destruction" (2 Thessalonians 1:9), a place where "the smoke of torment rises forever and ever" (Revelation 14:10-11), and a "lake of burning sulfur" where the wicked are "tormented day and night forever and ever" (Revelation 20:10).

The punishment of the wicked in hell is as never-ending as is the bliss of the righteous in heaven. Jesus himself indicates that punishment in hell is just as everlasting as life in heaven (Matthew 25:46). The wicked are forever subject to the fury and the wrath of God.

Those in hell will acknowledge the perfect justice of God (Psalm 76:10). Those who are in hell will know that their punishment is just and that they alone are to blame (Deuteronomy 32:3-5). Yes, hell is real. Yes, hell is a place of torment and punishment that lasts forever and ever, with no end. Praise God that, through Jesus, we can escape this eternal fate. (John 3:16, 18, 36) Excerpts from GotQuestions.org

Who Are The Wicked?

Will you be numbered with the wicked? Here is what the dictionary said about the word, "Wicked" (Highly offensive; obnoxious: a wicked stench.)

- **Adj. wicked** - morally bad in principle or practice.
- **evil** - morally bad or wrong; "evil purposes"; "an evil influence"; "evil deeds" **immoral** - deliberately violating accepted principles of right and wrong **impious** - lacking piety or reverence for a god.
- **wrong** - contrary to conscience or morality or law; "it is wrong for the rich to take advantage of the poor"; "cheating is wrong"; "it is wrong to lie."
- **unrighteous** - not righteous; "an unrighteous man"; "an unrighteous law."

The wicked are people that live in this lifestyle and practice it every day.

They violate the laws of God and rebel against his sovereign rule. They are their own god, doing what they want, not what God created them to be.

Here are a few scriptures related to the wicked and their wickedness.

Genesis 6:5 …And GOD saw that the wickedness of man was great in the earth, and that every imagination of the thoughts of his heart was only evil continually.

Genesis 38:7…And Er, Judah's firstborn, was wicked in the sight of the LORD; and the LORD slew him.

Chronicles 17:9… Also, I will ordain a place for my people Israel, and will plant them, and they shall dwell in their place, and shall be moved no more; neither shall the children of wickedness waste them anymore, as at the beginning,

Habakkuk 1:4 …Therefore the law is slacked, and judgment doth never go forth: for the wicked doth compass about the righteous; therefore, wrong judgment proceeded.

Malachi 3:18 …Then shall ye return, and discern between the righteous and the wicked between him that serves God and him that serves him not.

Psalms 101:8 …I will early destroy all the wicked of the land; that I may cut off all wicked doers from the city of the LORD.

Proverbs 21:12 …The righteous man wisely considers the house of the wicked: but *God* overthrows the wicked for their wickedness.

Proverbs 21:27 … The sacrifice of the wicked *is* abomination: how much more, *when* he bringeth it with a wicked mind?

Why Are The Fires of Hell Necessary?

The cleansing fire brings about a complete eradication of sin. Ezekiel 28:18-19 speaks the following about Satan: "Therefore I brought fire from your midst; it devoured you, and I turned you to ashes upon the earth…And (you) shall be no more forever." With Satan and all wickedness burned up, the Bible says that sin and affliction will never arise a second time. (Nahum 1:9)

Peter 3:10-14 explains that earth being on fire will melt, but that we should look forward to a new heaven and a new earth where righteousness dwells. The fire purifies the earth and establishes a place of righteousness for the saved to live. Isaiah 65:17 added, "For behold, I create new heavens and a new earth; and the former shall not be remembered or come to mind."

This righteous place is described in Revelation 21:1-5 in the following way: "Now I saw a new heaven and a new earth, for the first heaven and the first earth had passed away…And God will wipe away every tear from their eyes; there shall be no more death, nor sorrow, nor crying. There shall be no more pain, for the former things have passed away…Then he who sat on the throne said, 'behold, I make all things new.'"

The Reason Hell Was Created

In a relativistic culture, the very concept of sin must be defended vigorously. If morality is relative to each person, then there is no higher moral standard one can achieve or break.

But as C. S. Lewis argued in "*Mere Christianity*" and "*The Abolition of Man*", the idea of an objective moral law is inescapable. When we are snubbed or exploited, we call out for justice. When we encounter people of grit and grace, we praise them as moral examples. Our conscience is more than mere instinct or social conditioning. Yet because there is often a great gap between our ideals and actions, we suffer guilt and regret. Despite our denials and excuses, our consciences dog us throughout our days.

Christianity explains the global stain of human guilt by placing it in a theological framework that both sharpens its sting and makes relief possible. Sin is a moral condition that offends the holy God and removes us from his approval.

While much modern psychology assures us that guilt can be gutted through humanistic methods, the Gospel faces the problem head-on. Guilt is real because we have violated the standards of goodness. Left to ourselves, we can do nothing to undo our wrongs.

Forgiving ourselves is never sufficient because we are in no position to exonerate the guilty party — any more than a murderer can grant himself or herself a stay of execution.

Lawbreakers deserve punishment. But is hell too extreme? The great American theologian Jonathan Edwards took this question up in his essay, "The Justice of God in the Damnation of Sinners." Edwards argued that because God is "a Being of infinite greatness, majesty, and glory," He is therefore "infinitely honorable" and worthy of absolute obedience. "Sin against God, being a violation of infinite obligations, must be a crime infinitely heinous, and deserving of infinite punishment."

Edwards's much maligned but solidly Biblical sermon, "*Sinners in the Hands of an Angry God,*" presses home the point that without Christ, we have no grounds for confidence and every reason to fear hell. God, who is angry with sin, could justifiably send the unrepentant sinner to hell at any moment. Jesus himself warned, "Do not be afraid of those who kill the body but cannot kill the soul. Rather, be afraid of the one who can destroy both soul and body in hell" (Matt. 10:28).

To fathom the horror of sin and the holiness of God, we must kneel before the cross of Christ. While the Scriptures command us to be like Christ, this is never presented as the basis of our salvation. Christ's sinless perfection is impossible for us to attain, "for all have sinned and fall short of the glory of God" (Rom. 3:23). Because Jesus flawlessly obeyed God's moral law in our place, he is uniquely qualified to be our Savior. On the cross, Christ offered himself to the Father as a spotless sacrifice for our sin.

Sin against God is so severe that only the death of the sinless Son of God could atone for it. We see the reality of hell when the crucified Christ calls out, "My God, My God, why have you forsaken me?" (Mark 15:34). Paul explained, "God made him who had no sin to be sin for us, so that in him we might become the righteousness of God" (2 Cor. 5:21).

In the cross of Christ, the sinfulness of sin, the holiness of God, and the reality of hell are all seen through the blood of the Lamb. Only through Christ taking on our hell through his death could sinners be reconciled to a holy God. Once this is understood, hell takes on a clarity not otherwise perceived. Apart from the cross, there is no hope for forgiveness or reconciliation. Hell is the only alternative.

Only by understanding hell can we grasp the immensity of God's love. God's love took his Son to the hell of the cross for our sake. This is a costly love, a bloody love that has no parallel in any of the world's religions. Although other religions (particularly Islam) threaten hell, none offer the sure deliverance from it that Christianity offers through the sacrificial love of God himself.

(This article first appeared in the Effective Evangelism column of the CHRISTIAN RESEARCH JOURNAL, volume 19, number 03, 1997.)

For those who do not receive Jesus Christ as Savior, death means everlasting punishment (2 Thessalonians 1:8–9). There is no Biblical support for the notion that after death, people get another chance to repent. Hebrews 9:27 makes it clear that everyone dies physically and, after that, comes the judgment. Christians have already been judged and sentenced. Jesus took that sentence upon himself. Our sin becomes his and his righteousness becomes ours when we believe in him. Because he took our just punishment, we need not fear ever being separated from him again (Romans 8:29–30). The judgment for unbelievers is still to come.

"He will punish those who do not know God and do not obey the gospel of our Lord Jesus. They will be punished with everlasting destruction and shut out from the presence of the Lord and from the glory of his might." II Thessalonians. 1:8-9. The misery of hell will consist of not only physical torture but also the agony of being cut off from every avenue of happiness.

As I said before, God is the source of all good things (James 1:17). To be cut off from God is to forfeit all exposure to anything good. Hell will be a state of perpetual sin; yet those suffering there will possess full understanding of sin's horrors. Remorse, guilt, and shame will be unending, yet accompanied by the conviction that the punishment is just.

There will no longer be any deception about the "goodness of man." To be separated from God is to be forever shut off from light (1 John 1:5), love (1 John 4:8), joy (Matthew 25:23), and peace (Ephesians 2:14) because God is the source of all those good things. Any good we observe in humanity is merely a reflection of the character of God, in whose image we were created (Genesis 1:27).

While the spirits of those regenerated by God's Holy Spirit will abide forever with God in a perfected state (1 John 3:2), the opposite is true of those in hell. None of the goodness of God will exist in them. Whatever good they may have thought they represented on earth will be shown for the selfish, lustful, idolatrous thing it was (Isaiah 64:6). Man's ideas of goodness will be measured against the perfection of God's holiness and be found severely lacking. Those in hell have forever lost the chance to see God's face, hear His voice, experience His forgiveness, or enjoy his fellowship. To be forever separated from God is the ultimate punishment. (Taken from GotQuestions.com)

The Plan of Salvation Old And New Testament Saints

The Old Testament saints put their trust in, "The Coming One" Matt 11:2-7 And when John had heard in prison about the works of Christ, he sent two of his disciples and said to him, "Are You the Coming One, or do we look for another?" Jesus answers and said to them, "Go and tell John the things which you hear and see: the blind see and the lame walk; the lepers are cleansed and the deaf hear; the dead are raised up and the poor have the gospel preached to them. And blessed is he who is not offended because of Me." Isa. 29:18-19 "In that day the deaf shall hear the words of the book, And the eyes of the blind shall see out of obscurity and out of darkness. The humble also shall increase their joy in the LORD, And the poor among men shall rejoice in the Holy One of Israel. "

The Coming One

Many times, Jesus would make one statement and be quoting or hinting at four or five different verses in the Old Testament, especially when he was being attacked by the religious leaders, he would answer their questions with another question or statement that would allude to the scriptures that they were presuming to know so much about and following so closely. There are numerous examples but for now we will examine John's question and Jesus' response.

If we examine the Old Testament, we will find a multiplicity of statements about the Messiah being regarded as "The Coming One." In Hebrew, its "haba" which means "to come." One of the most popular "Messianic Scriptures" where this word is used is in one of the Psalms: Ps 118:26 "Blessed is he who comes in the name of the LORD!"

Another scripture in the Psalms that was regarded in Judaism as Messianic is in Psalm 40 where it contains the word "haba" spoken by Christ himself through David before Jesus was born: Ps 40:6-8 Sacrifice and offering You did not desire; My ears you have opened; Burnt offering and sin offering you did not require. Then I said, "Behold, I come; In the scroll of the book, it is written of me. I delight to do your will, O my God, and your law is within my heart."

Another example is found in the last book of our English Bible: Mal 3:1 "Behold, I send my messenger, and he will prepare the way before me. And the Lord, whom you seek, will suddenly come to his temple, even the messenger of the covenant, in whom you delight. Behold, he is coming," said the LORD of hosts.

The knowledge and expectation of the "Coming One" was prevalent during the time of Christ as we can see from a couple of examples:

John 6:14 "Then those men, when they had seen the sign that Jesus did, said, "This is truly the Prophet who is to come into the world."

John 11:25-27 Jesus said to her, "I am the resurrection and the life. He who believes in Me, though he may die, he shall live. And whoever lives and believes in me shall never die. Do you believe this?" She said to him, "Yes, Lord, I believe that You are the Christ, the Son of God, who is to come into the world."

Old Testament saints looked ahead to the "coming one". Their faith and hope were in him. The New Testament saints looked back to the cross, put their faith in the, "One who came." Messiah is a Hebrew term. It means, "Anointed." and Christ is a Greek term also meaning Anointed. Thus, both Old and New Testament saints put their trust and faith in the same Anointed One, sent from God. John 3:16 *His Name is Jesus, the Anointed One of God.*

Now all the folks that never heard of this "Anointed One", which Jesus proved that he was, fall into the Romans 2:14-15 "Salvation Net" that is stated above. All babies and children under the age of accountability are automatically saved because they have not willfully denied God's plan of salvation.

God does not want anyone to go to hell (2 Peter 3:9). That is why God made the ultimate, perfect, and sufficient sacrifice on our behalf. So, how can we not go to hell? Since only an infinite and eternal penalty is sufficient, an infinite and eternal price must be paid.

God became a human being in the person of Jesus Christ (John 1:1, 14). In Jesus Christ, God lived among us, taught us, and healed us—but those things were not his ultimate mission. God became a human being so that he could die for us. Jesus, God in human form, died on the cross.

As God, his death was infinite and eternal in value, paying the full price for sin (1 John 2:2). God invites us to receive Jesus Christ as Savior, accepting his death as the full and just payment for our sins. God promises that anyone who believes in Jesus (John 3:16), trusting him alone as the Savior (John 14:6), will be saved, i.e., not go to hell.

What about the Gentiles… (Everyone Else)

"For when the Gentiles, which have not the law, do by nature the things contained in the law, these, having not the law, are a law unto themselves: Which shew the work of the law written in their hearts, their conscience also bearing witness, and their thoughts the meanwhile accusing or else excusing one another" Romans 2:14-15 We have already discussed this in chapter five.

If you want this salvation, repent of your sin, and receive Jesus as your Savior. It is as simple as that. Tell God that you recognize you are a sinner and that you deserve to go to hell. Declare to God that you are trusting in Jesus Christ as your Savior. Thank God for providing for your salvation and deliverance from hell. Simple faith, trusting in Jesus Christ as the Savior, is how you can avoid going to hell!

CHAPTER SEVEN:
"HOW TO" SPOT HERESY IN THE CHURCH

Attaining the reality of God and enjoying it, now in this life, will take some smarts. You will need to avoid all the false doctrine and heresy floating around in this world's thinking.

This chapter will focus on heresy in the church. We will identify several heresies, their origins, their purpose, and the way to combat them. Our purpose is to make Christians aware of truth and error so they will not succumb to damnable heresies. We will also learn how to spot heretics and heretical doctrines.

The word, "Heresy" is defined by Webster's dictionary as; adherence to a religious opinion contrary to church dogma; dissent or deviation from a dominant theory, opinion, or practice; an opinion, doctrine, or practice contrary to the truth or to generally accepted beliefs or standards.

Heresy, according to Easton's Bible dictionary

Comes from a Greek word signifying (1) a choice, (2) the opinion chosen, and (3) the sect holding the opinion. In the Acts of the apostles (5:17; 15:5; Isaiah 24:5 Isaiah 24:14; 26:5) denoting a sect, without reference to its character.

Elsewhere, however, in the New Testament, it has a different meaning attached to it. Paul ranks "heresies" with crimes and seditions (Galatians

5:20). This word also denotes divisions or schisms in the church (1 Corinthians 11:19). In Titus 3:10, a "heretical person" is one who follows his own…self-willed "questions," and who is to be avoided.

Heresies thus came to signify self-chosen doctrines not emanating from God (2 Peter 2:1).

Where Does Heresy Come From?

Jesus said, "Beware of false prophets, which come to you in sheep's clothing, but inwardly they are ravening wolves. Ye shall know them by their fruits.

Do men gather grapes of thorns, or figs of thistles? Even so, every good tree bringeth forth-good fruit; but a corrupt tree bringeth forth-evil fruit. A good tree cannot bring forth evil fruit; neither can a corrupt tree bring forth good fruit. Every tree that bringeth not forth good fruit is hewn down, and cast into the fire."

Wherefore by their fruits ye shall know them. Matthew 7:15-20.

False Prophets Are anti-Christs

A false prophet is an anti-Christ. They can be pastors, teachers or just regular folk like you and me. However, they hold a private interpretation of the scriptures and use it to gather souls unto themselves. They make policy and doctrines that contradict the scriptures. They do this for their own gain.

Remember what Jesus said to his disciples on the Mount of Olives? "And Jesus answered and said unto them, take heed that no man deceives you. For many shall come in my name, saying, I am Christ; and shall deceive many." (Matthew 24: 4-5)

As I mentioned before, the word Christ is Greek for "Anointed One." I believe that Jesus was told his followers that as the world drew closer to its inevitable end that people would show up on the stage of life said, "I am anointed". It's another way of said I am a Christian. These professing Christians will deceive many with their damnable heresy. They will wear sheep's clothing. They will speak the lingo, and push their self-willed doctrines that do not line up with Biblical revelation.

Christianity is the most adhered religion in the United States, with 70.6% of polled American adults identifying themselves as Christian in 2014. This is down from 1965, where 93% identified themselves as Christian, according to the Pew Religious Report. These folks make up both Protestant and Catholic and every other sect claiming Christianity.

Let's talk for a moment about the many of Matthew 24 that are deceived. Who are these folks? I will list a few so you can see for yourself. all holds fast to a private interpretation: Mormonism, Unity Church, Christian Science, Jehovah's Witness and, well, you can fill in all the others. These claim to be children of God but deny or distort the gospel message of Christ. They do not believe in being "Born Again" as Jesus said in John chapter three, nor do they see salvation as being by grace.

To know them by their fruits is to listen to what they say about Christ and salvation. If it does not line up with what the apostles taught, they are false prophets. They are wolves in sheep's clothing.

Titles like pastor, evangelist, Bible teacher and the like mean nothing. We do not respect anyone that distorts the truth of God's Word. We are to turn away. We are the sheep of his pasture and hear only his voice.

Any spiritual minded believer would tell you that all of this is motivated by the devil. Jesus said, as recorded in John 10:10, "The thief cometh not, but for to steal, and to kill, and to destroy: I am come that they might have life, and that they might have it more abundantly."

Peter told the 1st century Christians to, "Be sober, be vigilant; because your adversary the devil, as a roaring lion, walketh about, seeking whom he may devour: Whom resist steadfast in the faith, knowing that the same afflictions are accomplished in your brethren that are in the world." I Peter 5:8-9.

It is obvious that these wolves in sheep's clothing are sent by Satan to deceive many, thereby stealing their destiny, destroying their peace in this world, and killing their dreams. We are admonished to resist using our faith in Christ and the Word of God.

The Purpose of Heresy

When Paul and Peter's writing began circulating, heresies were defined as a destructive element within the church that creates division through consciously formed opinions and ideas in disagreement with the orthodox teachings of the apostles. Paul condemns it in Galatians 5:20 as one of "the works of the flesh." Sometimes it is translated "factions" or "party spirit," but regardless of its translation, Paul said that people who practice such things will not inherit the kingdom of God (verse 21)! (Forerunner, February 1995) Thus, the purpose is to cause divisions and destroy established doctrine.

Heresy's Only Goal

The only goal is to lead the believer into error where he or she cannot benefit from the truth. A good example of this is in Galatians chapter three. (I have used this previously.)

"O foolish Galatians, who hath bewitched you, that ye should not obey the truth, before whose eyes Jesus Christ hath been evidently set forth, crucified among you? This only would I learn of you, Received ye the Spirit by the works of the law, or by the hearing of faith? Are ye so foolish? having begun in the Spirit, are ye now made perfect by the flesh? Have ye suffered so many things in vain? if it be yet in vain. He therefore that ministers to you the Spirit, and worketh miracles among you, doeth he it by the works of the law, or by the hearing of faith?" Galatians 3:1-5.

Paul called them foolish for starting out in the spirit and ending up in the flesh. That's what the devil wants….to take you away from living your life in the Spirit. He wants you to operate in the flesh so he can control you and torment you day and night.

The error was to dismiss *"Grace Through Faith"* and hold fast to salvation by works, which canceled out the finished work of Christ on the cross and positioned the believer to work at attaining salvation. No longer was it a free gift. Salvation by works is heresy for sure.

How Old Testament Saints Dealt with A False Profit

"If a prophet or a dreamer of dreams arises among you and gives you a sign or a wonder, and the sign or the wonder comes true, concerning which he spoke to you, saying, Let us go after other gods (whom you have not known) and let us serve them, you shall not listen to the words of that prophet or that dreamer of dreams; for the LORD your God is testing you to find out if you love the LORD your God with all your heart and with all your soul. (Did you catch that? God uses the false teaching to see if you mean what you say concerning him. He wants you to love him with all your heart and put him first in your life.)

You shall follow the LORD your God and fear him; and you shall keep his commandments, listen to his voice, serve him, and cling to him. But that prophet or that dreamer of dreams shall be put to death, because he has counseled rebellion against the LORD your God who brought you from the land of Egypt and redeemed you from the house of slavery, to seduce you from the way in which the LORD your God commanded you to walk So you shall purge the evil from among you." Deuteronomy 13:1-5.

How The Early Church Dealt with Heretical Teachings?

The Church fought against heresies from the very start. Here are some ways they attacked errors that crept into the church:

Acts 15:41 – The apostolic visits were solely to confirm or strengthen the church and ensure they are preserved from doctrinal errors.

1Cor. 1:11-13; 2: 1-2; Gal 3:1-3 – The epistles were written to various local assemblies to correct heresies and arrest the trend early.

1 Thess. 5: 2-8 – We are children of the day and not of the night, hence, let us keep the light of the true gospel shining. **Acts 15: 1-31**

1Tim. 1:3-7, 18 – Timothy was given specific charge when he was sent to Ephesus and this is to confront the heretical teachers.

2 Tim. 2:2; 4:2-5 – Paul advocates intentional mentoring as a way of dealing with wrong teachings. This approach will embolden true teachers of the Word to counter the effect of heretical teachings.

Tit.1:9-11 – The assignment of Titus among the Cretans was to stop the mouth of the false teachers.

1 John 2:15-19 – John warns against worldliness, as a sign of heretical teachings. He also identified the spirit at work as that of the antichrist.

How To Identify Heresy? (Gen 3:1-9)

- It appeals to the flesh – 2 Tim 4:2; 2 Pet 3:3.
- It challenges the authenticity of the Word of God.
- It is half-truth; just enough poison to damage the soul.
- It does not rely on the operation of the Holy Spirit.
- It could lead to a movement, but it will not produce true believers.
- It impoverishes the laity while the clergy lives big. – 1 Pet 5:2-3
- It feeds on the ignorance of the followers.
- It downplays end time warning – 2 Pet 3:3-4.

Heresy is a neighbor to apostasy. This is why there are homosexuals and lesbians who call themselves believers today.

A sure way to identify a false doctrine is to know the truth of God's Word. The 1st century believers studied, taught, fellowshipped, prayed, lived and died to ensure the decimation of the true doctrine of Christ. They risked everything for it. Nothing was compromised for the truth, 1 Tim 6:3-5; Rom 16: 17; Deut. 13:1-10, 2John 10-11. If you know the truth, not only will it set you free, but you will also be able to identify heresies afar off and help others to do the same. (Excerpts taken from RCCG SUNDAY SCHOOL, UK)

Damage Done By Heretical Teachings?

The biggest damage is divisiveness in the church. There are currently over 3,000 protestant denominations in the United States. Unity is a long way off as Christians fight over doctrines and church policies. Here are a few errors that are causing confusion and overshadow the truth of the apostolic doctrines:

- A shift from salvation by grace through faith to salvation by the works of the law.
- A shift from the eternal security of the believer to a loss of one's salvation due to falling short.
- A trend towards reincarnation as a means of getting better in degrees and thereby gaining salvation.
- A denial of God as the creator of all things, including man, for a theory of evolution.
- An assault on marriage as being holy and strictly for the benefit of male and female to being expanded to include same sex marriages. (The Methodist church is struggling with this right now and could split over the LGBTQ issue.
- A huge decline in the need to be, "Born Again" to enter the kingdom of God among self-identified protestant Christians.
- A significant rise in the belief that Jesus is no longer the only way to God the Father.
- The legalization of abortion and the murder of more than 50-million babies in their mother's womb.

I am sure you can think of more ways heresy has damaged the church and diluted the Christian faith. These are just a few.

Why Do We Still Tolerate Heresy?

Much of today's heresy started in the secular world. Over the years, Christians began to accept the false teachings until it has now become acceptable in most groups except the ultra-conservative. The government was and still is an agent of heresy as it pushes abortion rights and gay lifestyle through legislation.

Being politically correct is more important than Biblically sound. Churches now accept gays, tolerate immorality, and even embrace liberalism, all in an effort to not be ridiculed as a backward non-progressive institution. What was once light to the soul has become darkness in the eyes of the world, and the world's darkness is now light by which society defines itself.

Heresy In the Catholic Church

Here is a list of Catholic traditions that are contrary to Bible truth:

OF ALL THE HUMAN TRADITIONS taught and practiced by the Roman Catholic Church, which are contrary to the Bible, the most ancient are the **prayers for the dead** and the **sign of the Cross**. Both began around 300 years after Christ.

The **worship of Mary**, the mother of Jesus, and the use of the term, "Mother of God", as applied to her, originated in the Council of Ephesus around 431 A.D.

The doctrine of purgatory was first established by Gregory the Great in 593 A.D. The Bible teaches that we pray to God alone. In the primitive church, never were prayers directed to Mary, or to dead saints. This practice began in the Roman Church around 600 Ad. (Matthew 11:28; Luke 1:46; Acts 10:25-26;

14:14-18)

The Papacy is of pagan origin. The title of **"Pope"** or universal bishop, was first given to the bishop of Rome by the wicked emperor Phocas. This he did to spite Bishop Ciriacus of Constantinople, who had justly excommunicated him for his having caused the assassination of his predecessor emperor Mauritius. Gregory 1, then bishop of Rome, refused the title, but his successor, Boniface III, first assumed title "Pope" in 610 A.D. Jesus did not appoint Peter to the headship of the apostles and forbade any such notion. (Luke 22:24-26; Ephesians 1:22-23; Colossians 1:18; 1st Corinthians 3:11).

Note: Nor is there any mention in scripture, nor in history, that Peter ever was in Rome, much less that he was Pope there for 25 years; Clement, 3rd bishop of Rome, remarks that "there is no real 1st century evidence that Peter ever was in Rome."

Worship of the cross, images and relics was authorized in 788 A.D.. This was by order of Dowager Empress Irene of Constantinople, who first caused to pluck the eyes of her own son, Constantine VI, and then called a church council at the request of Hadrian I, pope of Rome at that time. Such practice is called simply IDOLATRY in the Bible and is severely condemned. (Read Exodus 20:4; 3:17; Deuteronomy 27:15; Psalm 115).

Canonization of dead saints, first by Pope John XV in 995 A.D. Every believer and follower of Christ is called a saint in the Bible. (Read Romans 1:7; 1st Colossians 1:2).

Fasting on Fridays and during **Lent** was imposed in 998 A.D. Imposed by Popes said to be interested in the commerce of fish. (Bull, or permit to eat meat), some authorities say, began in the year 700. This is against the plain teaching of the Bible. (Read Matthew 15:10; 1st Corinthians 10:25; 1st Timothy 4:1-3).

Pope Hildebrand, Boniface VII decreed the Celibacy of the Priesthood in 1079 A.D.. Jesus imposed no such rule, nor did any of the apostles. On the contrary. St. Peter was a married man, and St. Paul says that bishops were to have a wife and children. (Read 1st Timothy 3:2,5, and 12; Matthew 8:14-15).

The Rosary, or prayer beads was introduced by Peter the Hermit, in the year 1090. Copied from Hindus and Mohammedans. The counting of prayers is a pagan practice and is expressly condemned by Christ. (Matthew 6:5-13).

The dogma of Transubstantiation was decreed by Pope Innocent III, in the year 1215 A.D. By this doctrine the priest pretends to perform a daily miracle by changing a wafer into the body of Christ, and then he pretends to eat him alive in the presence of his people during Mass. The Bible condemns such absurdities; for the "Lord's Supper" is simply a memorial of the sacrifice of Christ. The spiritual presence of Christ is implied in the Lord's Supper. (Read Luke 22:19-20; John 6:35; 1st Corinthians 11:26).

Confession of sin to the priest at least once a year was instituted by Pope Innocent III., in the Lateran Council of 1215 A.D.. The Bible commands us to confess our sins directly to God. (Read Psalm 51:1-10; Luke 7:48; 15:21; 1st John 1:8-9).

The Bible is forbidden to laymen and placed in the Index of forbidden books by the Council of Valencia in 1229 A.D. Jesus commanded that the Scriptures should be read by all. (John 5:39; 1st Timothy 3:15-17).

The Council of Trent, held in the year 1545, declared that **"Tradition"** is of equal authority with the Bible. By tradition is meant human teachings. The Pharisees believed the same way, and Jesus bitterly condemned them, for by teaching human tradition, they nullified the commandments of God. (Read Mark 7:7-13; Colossians 2:8; Revelation 22:18).

The apocryphal books were added to the Bible also by the Council of Trent in 1545 A.D. These books were not recognized as canonical by the Jewish Church. (See Revelation 22:8-9).

The Creed of Pope Pius IV was imposed as the official creed 1560 years after Christ and the apostles. True Christians keep the Holy Scriptures as their creed. Hence, their creed is 1500 years older than the creed of Roman Catholics. (Read Galatians 1:8).

The **Immaculate Conception** of the "Virgin Mary" was proclaimed by Pope Pius IX in 1834. The Bible states that all men, except for Christ, are sinners. Mary herself had need of a Savior. (Read Romans 3:23; 5:12; Psalm 51:5; Luke 1:30,46,47).

In the year 1870 after Christ, Pope Pius IX proclaimed the dogma of **Papal Infallibility.** This is a blasphemy and the sign of the apostasy and of the antichrist predicted by St. Paul. (Read 2nd Thessalonians 2:2-12; Revelation 17:1-9; 13:5-8,18). Many Bible students see the number of the beast (Rev. 13:18), 666 in the Roman letters of the Pope's title: "VICARIVS FILII DEI." -- V-5, I-1; C-100, I-1; V-5, I-1; L-50, I-1; I-1; D-500, I-l — Total, 666.

In the year 1931 the same pope Pius XI, reaffirmed the doctrine that Mary is **"The Mother of God"**. This doctrine was first invented by the Council of Ephesus in the year 431. This is a heresy contrary by Mary's own words. (Read Luke 1:46-49; John 2: l-5).

In the year 1950 the last dogma was proclaimed by Pope Pius XII, the **Assumption of the Virgin Mary**

(Compiled by Rev. Stephen L. Testa)

Heresies In the Protestant Church

Here are a few false teachings that have crept into our protestant churches.

Salvation By Works...this false doctrine puts our eternal security on a foundation of good works. That is never enough to attain salvation. It also negates the finished work of Christ on the cross as the ultimate sacrifice for our sin. It also diminishes the concept of a free gift from God that came because of his matchless love for us, as declared in **John 3:16.**

The House of God Doctrine...this false teaching is that the brick-and-mortar building is the temple of God and that believers are to keep it holy and be there every time the doors open. Its teaching is that you meet God there, not on the streets of your city or in the quietness of your own heart.

This is contrary to I Cor. 6:19 which said, "What? know ye not that your body is the temple of the Holy Ghost which is in you, which ye have of God, and ye are not your own?" The correct theological view is that we, "all Born Again" believers, are the house of God. "Ye also, as lively stones, are built up a spiritual house, a holy priesthood, to offer up spiritual sacrifices, acceptable to God by Jesus Christ." (I Peter 2:5) Next time you go to church, call it a believer's fellowship, not the house of God. You are His house.

Mandatory Tithing…Tithing was exampled in the Old Testament but the New Testament teaches that we are a new creature in Christ and thus all that we are and have belongs to God. Matthew 16:24-26 said, "Then Jesus told his disciples, "If anyone would come after me, let him deny himself and take up his cross and follow me. For whoever would save his life will lose it, but whoever loses his life for my sake will find it. For what will it profit a man if he gains the whole world and forfeits his soul? Or what shall a man give in return for his soul?"

Rev. John Walvoord, a Christian theologian, pastor, and president of Dallas Theological Seminary from 1952 to 1986 had a right perspective. Here's what he said, (*Major Bible Themes,* Revised) Grand Rapids: Académie Books

"In matters pertaining to the giving of money, the grace principle involves the believer's recognition of God's sovereign authority over all that the Christian is and has, and contrasts with the Old Testament legal system of tithing which was in force as a part of the law until the law was done away with (John 1:16-17; Rom. 6:14; 7:1-6; 2 Cor. 3:1-18; Gal. 3:19-25; 5:18; Eph. 2:15; Col. 2:14).

Though certain principles of the law were carried forward and restated under grace, tithing, like the Sabbath observance, was never imposed on the believer in this dispensation. Since the Lord's Day superseded the legal Sabbath and is adapted to the principles of grace as the Sabbath could not be, so tithing has been superseded by a new system of giving which is adapted to the teachings of grace, as tithing could not be."

Their giving was not by commandment 1 Cor. 8:8, nor of necessity II Cor. 9:7. Under the law, a tenth was commanded and its payment was a necessity; under grace, God is not seeking the gift, but an expression of devotion from the giver. Under grace no law is imposed and no proportion to be given is stipulated, and, while it is true that God works in the yielded heart both to will and to do of his good pleasure (Phil. 2:13), he finds pleasure only in that gift which is given cheerfully, or more literally, "hilariously" (II Cor. 9:7)

The early Christians, first of all, gave themselves. Acceptable giving is preceded by a complete giving of oneself (II Cor. 8:5). God never imposed tithing on any other than the nation of Israel (Lev. 27:34; Num. 18:23-24; Mal. 3:7-10).

God sustains the giver. God will sustain grace giving with limitless temporal resources (II Cor. 9:8-10; Luke 6:38). In this connection it may be seen that those who give as much as a tenth are usually prosperous in temporal things, but since the believer can have no relation to the law (Gal. 5:1), it is evident that this prosperity is the fulfillment of the promise under grace, rather than the fulfillment of promises under the law. No blessings are thus dependent on exact tithing. Remember, Jesus said in Mathew 6:33 that these things, meaning stuff that the world seeks after, will be added to the believer as he seeks God and his righteousness. He did not say if you tithe 10%.

God loves a cheerful giver that offers his or her entire being and fortune. Grace giving is what God lays on your heart, not what an Old Testament law dictates. Does this then free the New Testament believer of any obligation to support God's work of grace? No, it does not. Grace giving frees the believer to *hear from God* and opens the door to giving what is placed upon his or her heart.

I realize that this teaching lends itself to a less than 10% tithe because of the greed of many or selfishness of some. However, it also promotes giving as a happy cheerful experience that is born out of a close walk with the Lord. We must first hear from God before we give. 10% can easily be an escape from having to hear from God. Remember, under grace, it all belongs to God. We are only Stewards of his blessings.

Man's Purpose Is Self-Determined… Most folks, even Christians, have very little understanding where they came from, why they are here and where they are going when they die. We are told that we need to find our slot in life, our purpose, as though it were a profession or job. Only then will we be happy and find peace. This is not in line with Biblical teaching.

God gave us our purpose in Genesis chapter one, **"To Be the Image of God"**, his very reflection on the earth. That is a lot different than being a Doctor, Marketing Director, or some other profession. His divine will, will prevail in leading us to a work-related job, if we listen to him and follow his lead. What we take with us along life's way is our character. If we are tuned into God's Spirit, allowing him to bring forth the life of Jesus in us, we will begin to manifest the fruit of the Spirit as shown in Galatians 5:22, "But the fruit of the Spirit is love, joy, peace, longsuffering, gentleness, goodness, faith, meekness, temperance: against such there is no law."

If we are filled with the Spirit, as we are commanded, (Ephesians 5:18), we will display Godly fruit in our lives. I believe that doing this is letting our light so shine as Jesus asked us to do. (Mathew 5:16)

Man of God Supremacy…this is a false teaching. It said that the pastor or some other church leader is the "Man of God" and therefore cannot be questioned. His word is final. This goes directly against the teaching in I Cor.12:7-11 that says,

"But the manifestation of the Spirit is given to every man to profit withal. For to one is given by the Spirit the word of wisdom; to another the word of knowledge by the same Spirit; to another faith by the same Spirit; to another the gifts of healing by the same Spirit; to another the working of miracles; to another prophecy; to another discerning of spirits; to another divers kinds of tongues; to another the interpretation of tongues: But all these worketh that one and the selfsame Spirit, dividing to every man severally as he will."

Husband Lordship… this false teaching puts the wife under the foot of her husband and encourages the male to dominate the female as though she were a 2nd class citizen. It goes against the Biblical teaching of Ephesians 5:22-33,

"Wives, submit yourselves unto your own husbands, as unto the Lord. For the husband is the head of the wife, even as Christ is the head of the church: and he is the savior of the body." *("Read On!")*

"Therefore, as the church is subject unto Christ, so let the wives be to their own husbands in everything. *Husbands, love your wives, even as Christ also loved the church, and gave himself for it;* That he might sanctify and cleanse it with the washing of water by the word, that he might present it to himself a glorious church, not having spot, or wrinkle, or any such thing; but that it should be holy and without blemish. So ought men to love their wives as their own bodies.

He that loveth his wife loveth himself. For no man ever yet hated his own flesh; but nourishes and cherishes it, even as the Lord the church: For we are members of his body, of his flesh, and of his bones. For this cause shall a man leave his father and mother, and shall be joined unto his wife, and they two shall be one flesh. his is a great mystery: but I speak concerning Christ and the church. Nevertheless, let every one of you in particular so love his wife even as himself; and the wife see that she reverences her husband."

Husbands and wives are to submit to one another in a bond of love. Yes, the husband is the head, but that headship is to lead from a position of love, counting on the wife for counsel as a helpmeet, knowing that he is not fully equipped to accomplish all that God wants for him.

We are all children of God; therefore, there is no need to be, "Born Again" …We are not all children of God. Listen to Paul as he writes to the church at Corinth. "2 Corinthians 6:14 - Be ye not unequally yoked together with unbelievers: for what fellowship hath righteousness with unrighteousness? and what communion hath light with darkness? Paul describes two types of folks: light and darkness.

The children of light are righteous (In Christ) while the children of the darkness are unrighteous (Dwelling in sin). Being a child of the darkness is to be a child of disobedience. "Wherein in time past ye walked according to the course of this world, according to the prince of the power of the air, the spirit that now worketh in the children of disobedience: Ephesians 2:2

Being "Born Again" is a prerequisite to salvation. You cannot enter God's kingdom without first being born again. See John chapter three.

The Gifts of the Holy Spirit ended with the death of the apostles… The biggest issue is found in speaking in tongues. This has divided many a fellowship. Some use the gift to edify themselves and communicate spirit to Spirit with God. Others insist that tongues, along with all the other gifts, were stopped with the death of the apostles, and this century has no need for them.

Here's some food for thought. (I've mentioned them before.)

- **The gifts validated Jesus' claim** that he was the Messiah, the Christ. They were bestowed upon his followers to continue that validation. Why would that not be needed now in our generation?
- **The gifts were given to the followers of Jesus** to help the body to grow and become one. The words of wisdom, knowledge, miracles, and even tongues were all aimed at bringing unity and purpose to God's people. Isn't that still needed in today's world?

- There are way more people in today's world, (20 times more), than back in Jesus' day. Isn't the need for Holy Spirit power through the gifts needed more now than ever before?
- The apostles laid hands on new believers, that were not apostles, and they received the gifts and began to operate in them. They were passed on and on from anointed believer to new convert. Why would that need to stop? **That which is perfect has not yet come.**

Satan's deception is obvious in this matter. He has deceived many in believing they do not need even one Holy Spirit gift because it is a thing of the past. This is a practical stripping of power and stealing of authority. If you do not believe that you can discern spirits, you'll never try. If you do not believe that God can and will give you a word of wisdom or a word of knowledge, you'll miss out on his will and end up groping in the dark for answers. The gifts are needed today more than ever before.

The Dangers of False Doctrines

(American Standard Version)

Ephesians 4:14 ..." We are no longer to be children, tossed here and there by waves and carried about by every wind of doctrine, by the trickery of men, by craftiness in deceitful scheming;"

1 Timothy 1:18-20 ..." This command I entrust to you, Timothy, my son, in accordance with the prophecies previously made concerning you, that by them you fight the good fight, keeping faith and a good conscience, which some have rejected and suffered shipwreck in regard to their faith. Among these are Hymenaeus and Alexander, whom I have handed over to Satan, so that they will be taught not to blaspheme."

2 Timothy 2:16-18..." But avoid worldly and empty chatter, for it will lead to further ungodliness, and their talk will spread like gangrene. Among them are Hymenaeus and Philetus, men who have gone astray from the truth saying that the resurrection has already taken place, and they upset the faith of some."

Titus 1:10-11…" For there are many rebellious men, empty talkers and deceivers, especially those of the circumcision, who must be silenced because they are upsetting whole families, teaching things they should not teach for the sake of sordid gain."

Hebrews 13:9 …" Do not be carried away by varied and strange teachings; for it is good for the heart to be strengthened by grace, not by foods, through which those who were so occupied were not benefited."

2 Peter 3:17 …" You therefore, beloved, knowing this beforehand, be on your guard so that you are not carried away by the error of unprincipled men and fall from your own steadfastness."

Romans 16:17-18 …" Now I urge you, brethren, keep your eye on those who cause dissensions and hindrances contrary to the teaching which you learned, and turn away from them. For such men are slaves, not of our Lord Christ but of their own appetites; and by their smooth and flattering speech they deceive the hearts of the unsuspecting."

Timothy 1:3-4 …" As I urged you upon my departure for Macedonia, remain on at Ephesus so that you may instruct certain men not to teach strange doctrines, nor to pay attention to myths and endless genealogies, which give rise to mere speculation rather than furthering the administration of God which is by faith."

Galatians 1:8-9…" But even if we, or an angel from heaven, should preach to you a gospel contrary to what we have preached to you, he is to be accursed! As we have said before, so I say again now, if any man is preaching to you a gospel contrary to what you received, he is to be accursed!"

Peter 2:1… "But false prophets also arose among the people, just as there will also be false teachers among you, who will secretly introduce destructive heresies, even denying the Master who bought them, bringing swift destruction upon themselves." (Excerpts from Knowing Jesus.com)

Biblical Warnings About Counterfeits

- **John 4:1…** "Beloved, do not believe every spirit, but test the spirits to see whether they are from God, because many false prophets have gone out into the world." ASV
- **Corinthians 11:13 …** "For such men are false apostles, deceitful workers, disguising themselves as apostles of Christ."
- **Matthew 24:23-24…** "Then if anyone said to you, Behold, here is the Christ, or 'There he is,' do not believe him. For false Christs and false prophets will arise and will show great signs and wonders, so as to mislead, if possible, even the elect."
- **Galatians 1:6-7 …** "I am amazed that you are so quickly deserting him who called you by the grace of Christ, for a different gospel; which is really not another; only there are some who are disturbing you and want to distort the gospel of Christ." ASV
- **Corinthians 11:13 …** "For such men are false apostles, deceitful workers, disguising themselves as apostles of Christ."

Finally, avoid the centuries old controversy between Calvinism and Arameanism. The subject is too confusing to go into now. However, it is enough to say that the subject involves limited atonement, loss of salvation, unconditional election, and a lot more that is against Bible doctrine. See my new book, It's Your Choice, or Is It" coming out in March or April of 2024 for a full discussion on this subject.

It should be noted that heresy is not restricted to religion. It is a contrary opinion or set of rules that go against an established doctrine. In the above cases, the disregard for original Biblical truth makes it a heresy. The fact that the 1st apostles, who walked with and were taught by Jesus, fought against most of these heresies proves that what was being introduced to the church as a new doctrine was false.

As I have mentioned previously, the best way to not get caught up in false teachings is to know the truth. It will set you free and keep you in the Will of God.

One last comment…**Colossians 2:8**… Beware lest any man spoil you through philosophy and vain deceit, after the tradition of men, after the rudiments of the world, and not after Christ.

Remember, chapter seven is all about spotting heresy in the church. It is a reality that we cannot consider or even indulge. "Reality Squared" is God's reality, not all these false teachings.

CHAPTER EIGHT:
"HOW TO" LIVE OUT YOUR DIVINE DESTINY

Finally, we will look at how we, as Christians, can live out our divine destiny. I offer this as a "Reality Squared" solution that will take us into the reality of God.

Finding God's Will for Your Life

This chapter helps believers find and maintained the, "Will of God", for their lives. What to do in certain situations is vital to pleasing the Lord and living an abundant life. This is yet another "Reality Squared" adventure.

I will share specific scriptures that will erase any doubts that may arise concerning God's Will for his children. I hope every reader will walk away with a clear perspective of who God really is, his destiny for his children, and the principles that take us into God's presence and keep us in his will. This is another "Reality Squared" teaching.

When I was a young Christian, I wished with all my heart that I could actually know the will of God. I often sent up prayers to heaven and said, "Lord, what do I do now?" It got so bad that I could hardly drive my car because I could not decide if God wanted me in the left or right lane on a 4-lane highway.

Months went by with my continual prayers to God that shouts into heaven, *"What Do I Do Now?"* Finally, I was invited to a Bible study, started going to church and began reading my Bible. The answers came ever so slow but fast enough for me to digest and store them away in my heart.

Now, after 60+ years of Bible study, prayer, and life-application, I can said with confidence that I do know and understand "God's Will." I am still learning and studying and applying. I even, at times, asked myself, "Why didn't I see that before now?"

I am going to open your eyes if you are blind, refresh your spirit if it is weary and strengthen your personal walk with Jesus, our Lord & Savior, by providing the tools needed to keep you keeping on. **Hang on!** It's sure to be an exciting adventure.

Knowing That You Know

If you call yourself a "Child of God", you should agreed with me that you ought to know the Will of your Heavenly Father. You are openly admitting to a relationship and claiming family rights and access. Are we in agreement so far?

Knowing God is a logical assumption when we claim to be his child. Yet most of the Christians I know have serious doubts about the "Will of God" for them. This can only mean one of two things:

Your relationship with God the Father is not a close one. You pray, he listens, but you rarely feel his presence or hear his voice, or you have claimed to be a child of God but really are not. You know there is something not right but are too ashamed or afraid to openly admit to not being a child of God.

In either case mentioned above, there is a way to *"know that you know"* so there is no more doubt. However, knowing that you know takes "Faith." God is speaking all the time through the Bible, through his Spirit and through other folks that he brings into your life. The quick fix to *"Knowing That You Know"* is to *"Listen and Believe"*. You cannot live out your divine destiny if you do not know the will of God.

I can say, without a doubt, that I know the Will of God for my life. I can make such a claim because God, my Heavenly Father, has published 66 books that contain over 3,000 promises and many great statements as to what his will is for his children. It's all there in the Bible, just waiting for me to dig it out.

To know that you know is a great feeling because there is no more anxiety. I know and have been persuaded that this way is the right way and my new perspective (Point of View) brings me a lot of comfort, peace and hope for the future.

"And thine ears shall hear a word behind thee, saying, this *is* the way, walk ye in it, when ye turn to the right hand, and when ye turn to the left." Isaiah 30:21.

The Bible said, "For ye have not received the spirit of bondage again to fear; but ye have received the Spirit of adoption, whereby we cry, **Abba, Father**. The Spirit itself *bears witness* with our spirit that we are the children of God: And if children, then heirs; heirs of God, and joint-heirs with Christ; if so be that we suffer with him, that we may be also glorified together**.**" Romans 8:15-17.

As the scripture says, the Spirit of God will bear witness with our spirits that we are the children of God. If you have even felt, seen or otherwise realized the witness of God's Spirit, you will know without a shadow of a doubt that you are a child of God…. And if a child also a joint heir with Christ.

How Does the Holy Spirit Bear Witness with Our Spirit?

Notice that the apostle Paul did not say that the Spirit bears witness with our flesh, our souls, or minds. He did not say the witness would be through the intellect. He said the witness would be from Spirit to spirit. That means it could be one of many gentle quiet assurances that we did the right thing at the right time. It could be a sense of stability when things are going rough. It could be an "I just know" feeling.

The point here is that God's Spirit is talking to us and our spirit is listening and rejoicing that it can hear God when he speaks. One definite witness, that I can recall, is when I first started reading the scriptures, they started jumping off the page with new and fresh revelation. The Bible suddenly came alive and spoke directly to my spirit. God's Holy Spirit was and is still confirming to me that I am a child of the living God. His witness is a continual thing. It goes on as long as we have breath.

So, we have a quiet assurance and a loud voice that calls us to the Word of God, where we receive faith, instruction, assurance, strength, knowledge, and a lot more. God's witness is everywhere.

It's Not Rocket Science

Finding God's will is not rocket-science. We have already learned that God's Holy Spirit is available to confirm or excuse our decisions in life. We also know that it is our" Free Will" that engages truth and activates faith to empower us to walk in the Spirit.

The key to *"Knowing That You Know"* is absolute submission to his will. Here's what Jesus said, "If any man will do his will, (God's Will), he shall know of the doctrine, whether it be of God, or whether I speak of myself." John 17:7.

We must be ready and willing to do his will. When we are, we will know the doctrine or revelation knowledge necessary to accomplish the revealed will of God.

Question! Why should God give us the knowledge of his will if we are not willing or not ready to use it? That would be a waste of time and energy on God's part and, in my opinion, he just doesn't operate that way.

He has, however, already revealed his Will in the pages of the Bible. If we really want to know, we can read and discover and learn and apply all that God has for us? So, let's look at the Bible.

I will take you on a journey so you can discover some of the great and precious promises that prove out what the Will of God is. We will look at several scriptures and discuss them.

God's Divine Will As Revealed In The Bible

"And God said, let us make man in our image, after our likeness: and let them have dominion over the fish of the sea, and over the fowl of the air, and over the cattle, and over all the earth, and over every creeping thing that creeps upon the earth." Genesis 1:26.

God wanted to create man (Male & Female). his divine will was to create us. He did that in his likeness and image. Then he gave us dominion over the earth and all its life forms. What does this say to us? Simply this, we were not a mistake, after thought or freak mutation of nature by evolution over millions of years. We were a specific, deliberate design to accomplish the goals and objectives of God in the earth.

" And let them have dominion" Genesis 1:26 The word, "Them" is all of us. We were to rule as the "Head" and not the Tail.

Now, let's proceed on our journey to discover the revealed "Will of God."

Revelation #1…God's will for our lives is to take dominion over evil and live in such a way as to reveal the image and likeness of God.

Man Is Created Male & Female

Genesis 2:18-25 is the Biblical record of God creating woman as a helper for Adam. "And the LORD God said, it is not good that the man should be alone; I will make him a helper suitable for him."

"And the LORD God caused a deep sleep to fall upon Adam, and he slept: and he took one of his ribs, and closed up the flesh instead thereof; And the rib, which the LORD God had taken from man, made he a woman, and brought her unto the man. And Adam said, this *is* now bone of my bones, and flesh of my flesh: she shall be called Woman, because she was taken out of man.

Therefore, shall a man leave his father and his mother, and shall cleave unto his wife: and they shall be one flesh. And they were both naked, the man and his wife, and were not ashamed." *Our creation was and is still God's Will.*

Revelation #2… It is God's Will for a man to have a woman at his side. God ordained marriage and joined them together. Where does this leave homosexuality? It was never in the will of God.

Revelation #3… God's greatest creation, (humanity), fell into sin and is now in need of a Savior.

The Fall of Man…Death In Adam, Life In Christ

(Genesis 3:1-7; Genesis 7:1-5; 2 Peter 3:1-9)

" Wherefore, as by one man sin entered into the world, and death by sin; and so death passed upon all men, for that all have sinned: (For until the law sin was in the world: but sin is not imputed when there is no law. Nevertheless, death reigned from Adam to Moses, even over them that had not sinned after the similitude of Adam's transgression, who is the figure of him that was to come." Romans 5:12-14)

Romans 5:18-21 told us, "Therefore as by the offence of one (Adam) *judgment came* upon all men to condemnation; even so by the righteousness of one (Jesus) *the free gift came* upon all men unto justification of life. 19- For as by one man's disobedience many were made sinners, so by the obedience of one shall many be made righteous. Moreover, the law entered, that the offence might abound. But where sin abounded, grace did much more abound: That as sin hath reigned unto death, even so might grace reign through righteousness unto eternal life by Jesus Christ our Lord."

Man falls from God's reality into the reality of darkness or sin. His free will choice changed his destiny. He lost the image and likeness of God. But God still loves him and has a plan for his restoration. *Man is justified by the blood of Jesus. His righteousness was imparted to us, that is, all who believe.*

Revelation #4…God loves us and does not want us to perish.

Jesus said, "For God so loved the world, that he gave his only begotten Son, that whosoever believeth in him should not perish, but have everlasting life." John 3:16 states that whoever believes in Jesus is given eternal life.

"But God commended his love toward us, in that, while we were yet sinners, Christ died for us." Romans 5:8 He died for us that we might live for him. (*This is the foundation of the Gospel of Jesus Christ.*)

Revelation #5…God wants us to repent and accept Jesus as our Savior so we can live in relationship with him.

"The Lord is not slack concerning his promise, as some men count slackness; but is longsuffering to us-ward, *not willing that any should perish, but that all should come to repentance.*" II Peter 2:9 We must repent of our sin because salvation is essential to knowing God's Will.

Revelation #6…God wants us to live life with a thankful heart. This allows God to be God over us and allows us to express our dependence upon him. It also relieves us from the burden and stress of being our own god. *We don't have to be in control of everything.*

Give Thanks in Everything

"In everything, give thanks: for this is the will of God in Christ Jesus concerning you." I Thessalonians 5:17

The Bible is filled with commands to give thanks to God (Psalm 106:1; 107:1; 118:1; 1 Chronicles 16:34; 1 Thessalonians 5:18). Most verses go on to list reasons why we should thank him, such as "His love endures forever" (Psalm 136:3), "He is good" (Psalm 118:29), and "His mercy is everlasting" (Psalm 100:5). Thanksgiving and praise always go together. *We cannot adequately praise and worship God without also being thankful.*

Having feelings and expressing appreciation is good for us. Like any wise father, God wants us to learn to be thankful for all the gifts he has given us (James 1:17). It is in our best interest to be reminded that everything we have is a gift from him. Without gratefulness, we become arrogant and self-centered. We begin to believe that we have achieved everything on our own. *Thankfulness keeps our hearts in the right relationship to God, the giver of all good gifts.*

Giving thanks also reminds us of how much we have. Human beings are prone to covetousness. We tend to focus on what we don't have. By giving thanks continually, we are reminded of how much we do have. When we focus on blessings rather than wants, we are happier. When we thank God for the things we usually take for granted, our perspective changes. We realize we could not even exist without the merciful blessings of God." (Excerpts from www.gotquestions.org)

Revelation #7…God is worthy of our trust and when we trust in, rely upon and adhere to his voice, he will direct our paths.

Proverbs 3:5-6 offers another "Will of God" Revelation. "Trust in the LORD with all thine heart; and lean not unto thine own understanding. In all thy ways acknowledge him, and he shall direct thy paths."

Why should we trust the Lord? Many Christians ask that question because of adverse situations they are in or have gone through. Here are a few reasons:

- **God is not a liar**. He will always deal with us from a vantage point of truth.
- **God is immutable**, which means, he can never change. He does not say one thing and do another. When he speaks… Well, listen to how Isaiah put it…" *So shall my word be that goes forth out of my mouth: it shall not return unto me void, but it shall accomplish that which I please, and it shall prosper in the thing whereto I sent it." Isaiah 55:11.*

- **God is Love**… This can only mean that he has no hate in him. His war and revenge are against his enemies who walk in darkness, steal, kill and destroy. His children are the *"Apple of his Eye"* and the *"Subject of his Grace.*
- **God is our Protector**…" The angel of the LORD encamps round about them that fear him, and delivers them." Psalm 34:7.
- **God really does care for us**…" Casting all your care upon him; for he cares for you." I Peter 5:7 "Cast thy burden upon the LORD, and he shall sustain thee: he shall never suffer the righteous to be moved**.**" Psalm 55:22.
- **God is a God of Blessings, Not Curses**… (Psalms 1:1-3) "Blessed is the man who walks not in the counsel of the ungodly, nor stands in the path of sinners, nor sits in the seat of the scornful; But his delight is in the law of the LORD, and in his law, he meditates day and night. He shall be like a tree planted by the rivers of water, that brings forth its fruit in its season, whose leaf also shall not wither; And whatever he does shall prosper.
- **God is a God of Peace**…. "And the God of peace shall bruise Satan under your feet shortly. The grace of our Lord Jesus Christ be with you. Amen." Romans 16:20.

Because of who he is, we can, with confidence, acknowledge him, trust him, disregard our own feelings and follow his lead. He will always direct our paths.

Revelation #8… God wants to bring us back to where he had originally intended us to be. That place was in his image. Thus, he speaks through the pages of the Bible, letting us know he wants us to set ourselves apart for fellowship with him.

"For this is the will of God, even your sanctification, that ye should abstain from fornication:" I Thessalonians 4:3

The generic meaning of sanctification is *"the state of proper functioning."* To sanctify someone or something is to set that person or thing apart for the use intended by its designer. A pen is "sanctified" when used to write. Eyeglasses are "sanctified" when used to improve sight. In the theological sense, things are sanctified when they are used for the purpose God intended.

The Greek word translated "sanctification" means "holiness." To sanctify, therefore, means "to make holy." In one sense, only God is holy (Isa 6:3). God is separate, distinct, and there is no other. No human being or thing shares the holiness of God's essential nature. There is one God. Yet scripture speaks about holy things. Moreover, God calls human beings to be "holyas" or holy as he is holy (Lev 11:44; Matt 5:48; 1 Peter 1:15- 16). Another word for a holy person is "saint," meaning a sanctified one. The opposite of sanctified is "profane" (Lev. 10:10).

The imperfect state of creation is a reminder that God's fully sanctified purpose for it has been disrupted by sin. Evil is the deprivation of the good that God intended for the creation he designed.

"The creature itself also shall be delivered from the bondage of corruption into the glorious liberty of the children of God. For we know that the whole creation groans and travails in pain together until now." (Rom 8:21-22; Rev. 20-21). *Creation is awaiting its sanctification when everything will be set right.*

Human beings, made in God's image, were the pinnacle and focus of his creation. The sanctification of human beings, therefore, is the highest goal of God's work in the universe. God explicitly declared it to be his will (1 Thess 4:3). He purposed human beings would be "like him" in a way no other created thing is.

Human beings are like God in their stewardship over creation (Gen 1:26-31). Yet this role depends on a more fundamentally important likeness to God-moral character. By virtue of God-given discretionary autonomy (faith), human beings may so depend upon God that his moral character (communicable attributes) are displayed. (Dictionaries – Baker's Evangelical Dictionary of Biblical Theology–Sanctification)

We can never be holy in ourselves as he is holy but by faith, we can become the very righteousness of God in Jesus Christ. "For he hath made him to be sin for us, who knew no sin; that we might be made the righteousness of God in him**."** II Corinthians 5:21.

Revelation #9… God wants us to allow the mind of Christ to dwell in our hearts.

This is a voluntary act of humility and servitude to God the Father. It is the only way that we can be highly exalted with Christ.

" Let this mind be in you which was also in Christ Jesus, who, being in the form of God, did not consider it robbery to be equal with God, but made himself of no reputation, taking the form of a bondservant, and coming in the likeness of men. And being found in appearance as a man, he humbled himself and became obedient to the point of death, even the death of the cross.

Therefore, God also has highly exalted him and given him the name which is above every name, that at the name of Jesus every knee should bow, of those in heaven, and of those on earth, and of those under the earth, that every tongue should confess that Jesus Christ is Lord, to the glory of God the Father." Philippians 2:5-11

Note: Jesus had to be obedient unto death…this is his own will. Then he had to be obedient unto the death imposed upon him by the cross. We are not being asked to face the two deaths that Jesus had to endure. God only asked us to die to ourselves. Our will must die so his can become alive in us. We are not God's sacrifice for sin. Jesus is. We are a living sacrifice unto God that is to be conformed to the image of Christ. (Romans Chapter 12)

Revelation #10…God wants his peace to rule or referee in our hearts.

"And let the peace of God rule in your hearts, to the which also ye are called in one body; and be ye thankful." Colossians 3:15.

The word "Rule" in verse 15 expresses the intent to "Reign". It also can be interpreted as "Referee" as in a game. Paul is telling the church to allow the peace of God to referee any and all situations as though they were a game. By doing so, you can use God's peace as a referee's whistle. It will blow with anxiety, confusion, worry and so on to let you know that you are off sides and in need of a reconnect with the Holy Spirit to attain his peace and sustain an attitude of thankfulness.

If you find yourself in anger, worry or any other such attitude, you can automatically know that you have lost God's peace. God wants you to walk and live in his peace so you do not have to experience all that jazz of the flesh. It will kill you if left unattended.

Revelation #11…God wants us to prove what is the good, and perfect will of God.

" And be not conformed to this world: but be ye transformed by the renewing of your mind, that ye may prove what is that good, and acceptable, and perfect, will of God." Romans 12:1

We cannot allow non-believers to define what is or is not the acceptable or perfect Will of God. We need to be the Bible that they will not read. We need to demonstrate what good is and what perfect is so others around us can see the perfect will of God. The only way to get the job done is to reject the pull of this world into all its sin and be transformed in our minds so we do not fall for the wiles of the devil.

How do we renew our minds? By transforming your own mind from always thinking evil to allowing the mind of Christ to dwell in you. He will do the rest. Your mission is to not be conformed to this world but to align yourself with God's Will.

Revelation #12… God wants us to put on the whole armor of God so the devil cannot hurt us.

"Finally, my brethren, be strong in the Lord, and in the power of his might. Put on the whole armor of God, that ye may be able to stand against the wiles of the devil. For we wrestle not against flesh and blood, but against principalities, against powers, against the rulers of the darkness of this world, against spiritual wickedness in high places. Wherefore take unto you the whole armor of God, that ye may be able to withstand in the evil day, and having done all, to stand." Ephesians 6:10-13

Our fight is with the rulers of darkness. We are fighting because we need to defend ourselves. If we don't, we will become open game for the devil. Again, hear what Peter says in I Peter 5:8-9,

"Be sober, be vigilant; because your adversary the devil, as a roaring lion, walketh about, seeking whom he may devour: Whom resist steadfast in the faith, knowing that the same afflictions are accomplished in your brethren that are in the world."

Revelation #13…God wants us to guard our hearts with all diligence.

"Keep your heart with all diligence; for out of it are the issues of life." Proverbs 4:23 To keep one's heart is to guard it with all diligence. It implies that we should act as a gatekeeper that allows good things in and bad things from getting in. God wants us to protect our spiritual growth and resources. They can be depleted and even stolen by the devil.

Revelation #14…God wants us to pray without ceasing.

"Rejoice always, pray without ceasing, give thanks in all circumstances; for this is the will of God in Christ Jesus for you." I Thessalonians 5:16-18.

We pray without ceasing when we start our day talking to God and maintain an atmosphere of prayer all day. We rejoice and give thanks along the way, and life flows along like a calm, gentle sea.

Revelation #15…God Wants Us To Have Fellowship With Him.

"That which was from the beginning, which we have heard, which we have seen with our eyes, which we have looked upon, and our hands have handled, of the Word of life." I John 1:1

This simple and bold statement means that one can have a relationship with God. This idea would surprise many of John's readers, and it should be astounding to us. The Greek mindset highly prized the idea of fellowship, but restricted to men among men – the idea of such an intimate relationship with God was revolutionary.

Jesus started the same kind of revolution among the Jews when he invited men to address God as Father (Matthew 6:9). We really can have a living, breathing relationship with God the Father, and with Jesus Christ. He can be not only our Savior but also our counselor and our closest friend.

For many people, this is unappealing. Sometimes it is because they do not know who God is, and an invitation to a "personal relationship with God" is about as attractive to them as told an eighth-grader they can have a "personal relationship with the assistant principal." But when we know the greatness, the goodness, and the glory of God, we want to have a relationship with him.

Other people turn from this relationship with God because they feel so distant from him. They want a relationship with God, but feel so disqualified, so distant. They need to know what God has done to make this kind of relationship possible.

John identified this eternally existent being, who was physically present with John and others as the "Word of Life." This is the same "Logos" spoken of in John 1:1.

The idea of the Logos–of the Word–was important for John and for the Greek and Jewish worlds of his day. In the Jewish belief, God was often called the Word because they held the belief that God perfectly revealed himself in his Word. For the Greek, their philosophers had spoken for centuries about the Logos–the basis for organization and intelligence in the universe, the ultimate reasoning that controls all things.

It is as if John said to everyone, "This Logos you have been talking about and writing about for centuries – well, we have heard him, seen him, studied him, and touched him. Let me now tell you about him."

This life was manifested, meaning that it was made actually and physically real. John testified as an eyewitness (*we have seen, and bear witness, and declare to you*) that this was the case. This was no fairy tale, no "Once upon a time" story. This was real, and John tells us about it as an eyewitness. (Excerpts from David Guzik article on Fellowship with God)

Revelation #16…God Wants Us To Seek His Kingdom First, Above All Else In Life.

"But seek ye first the kingdom of God, and his righteousness; and all these things shall be added unto you." Matthew 6:33.

Jesus said to seek first the kingdom of God in his sermon on the mount (Matthew 6:33). The verse's meaning is as direct as it sounds. We are to seek the things of God as a priority over the things of the world. Primarily, it means we are to seek the salvation that is inherent in the kingdom of God because it is of greater value than all the world's riches.

Does this mean that we should neglect the reasonable and daily duties that help sustain our lives? Certainly not. But for the Christian, there should be a difference in attitude toward them. If we are taking care of God's business as a priority—seeking his salvation, living in obedience to him and sharing the good news of the kingdom with others—then he will take care of our business as he promised, and if that's the arrangement, where is worrying?

But how do we know if we are truly seeking God's kingdom first? There are questions we can ask ourselves.

"Where do I primarily spend my energies? Is all my time and money spent on goods and activities that will certainly perish, or in the services of God—the results of which live on for eternity?" Believers who have learned to truly put God first may then rest in this holy dynamic: "…and all these things will be given to you as well."

God has promised to provide for his own, supplying every need ***(Philippians 4:19)***, but his idea of what we need is often different from ours, and his timing will only occasionally meet our expectations.

A growing number of false teachers are gathering followers under the message, "God wants you to be rich!" But that philosophy is not the counsel of the Lord. It is certainly not the counsel of Matthew 6:33, which is not a formula for gaining wealth. It is a description of how God works. Jesus taught that our focus should be away from this world—its status and its lying allurements—and placed upon the things of God's kingdom. (Excerpts from gotquestions.org)

Matthew 6:33 is a call to priorities. We are invited to have fellowship with Christ but not in the appetites of sinful flesh. He wants us to walk with him in his kingdom. Jesus says that if we sell out to him, he will provide for us but if our selling out is to get rich, we have missed it before we start. God certainly wants us to prosper and be in good health but not by manipulation or exultation of self.

Revelation #17…God wants us to be filled with his Holy Spirit

"And be not drunk with wine, wherein is excess; but be filled with the Spirit; speaking to yourselves in psalms and hymns and spiritual songs, singing and making melody in your heart to the Lord;" Ephesians 5:18-19

This scripture clearly reveals God's will for his followers: Don't get drunk, be filled and sing. I want to focus more closely on being filled with the Spirit. I know that some of this was discussed in chapter three, but now I need to delve deeper so you can fully understand the scope of its reality. It is another "Reality Squared."

I am sure you will agreed that he is not referring to the spirit of evil or the human spirit of which we are already absorbed. It is obvious that the Spirit we need to be filled with is none other than the Spirit of the Lord.

How does one get filled with God's Spirit? The text here uses Greek words that mean to be continually filled as though it were possible to use up the Spirit and find yourself to be empty. I think many Christians are running on empty and are in serious need of a fill-up.

Paul wrote: "Do not get drunk on wine, which leads to debauchery. Instead, be filled with the Spirit." In the original Greek, the phrase "be filled: is a present-tense verb.

The word filling seems awkward when referring to the Holy Spirit's entrance into our lives. The Spirit of God is not a liquid, like water. He does not fill a person the way cold milk fills a cup. The Holy Spirit is God—he is one in essence with the Father and the Son—but he is also a distinct personality and has all the attributes thereof. That is why we refer to the Holy Spirit as the third person of the Trinity. Many scripture passages point to these facts.

Like a person, the Holy Spirit searches, helps, and guides. He knows; He feels; He wills. Scripture speaks of the Holy Spirit's mind, his love, and his instruction. In Ephesians 4:30, Paul wrote: "Do not grieve the Holy Spirit of God, with whom you were sealed for the day of redemption." The only way we can grieve someone is if the one we are grieving has feelings.

Because the Holy Spirit is a personality, it makes more sense to talk about the Spirit's control or compulsion in our lives, rather than his filling of our lives. Holy Spirit-driven is a good way to look at our response to his control.

A person who is filled with the Spirit is driven by the Spirit—driven in a gentle, loving way. A Spirit-driven person allows the Holy Spirit to direct and guide every decision.

Because the world, the flesh and the devil oppose the Spirit-controlled lifestyle, we need to be filled and renewed continually. (Excerpts taken from Joel Comiskey's article CBN.org.)

Baptism with the Holy Spirit or in the Holy Spirit in Christian theology is a term describing baptism (washing or immersion) in or with the Spirit of God and is frequently associated with the bestowal of spiritual gifts and empowerment for Christian ministry. (Acts 1:5,8)

To illustrate, consider this…if we drink water from a glass, then the water would be inside us. However, if we went to the beach and stepped into the ocean, then we would be in the water. We receive, as it were, a drink of the Holy Spirit when we are saved, but when we are "Baptized in the Spirit", it is as if that initial drink becomes an ocean that surrounds us. (A river of living water gushing up and overflowing everywhere.) "He that believeth on me, as the scripture hath said, out of his belly shall flow rivers of living water." John 7:38.

Just as the indwelling Spirit that Christians receive when they are saved reproduces the life of Jesus, so the outpouring, or baptizing by the Spirit reproduces the ministry of Jesus, including miracles and healings.

When Jesus gave the "Great Commission" (Matthew 28:19-20), He knew that his disciples could not fulfill it in their own power. Therefore, he had a special gift in store for them: It was his plan to give them the same power that he had – the power of the Spirit of God. So, immediately after giving them the "Great Commission", Jesus commanded his disciples not to leave Jerusalem, but to wait for what the Father promises, "which," he said, "you heard of from Me; for John baptized with water, but you shall be baptized with the Holy Spirit not many days from now" (Acts 1:4-5). He further promised: "You shall receive power when the Holy Spirit has come upon you; and you shall be my witnesses both in Jerusalem, and in all Judea and Samaria, and even to the remotest part of the earth" (Acts 1:8).

The disciples waited in Jerusalem as Jesus had commanded, and when they were all together, suddenly there came from heaven a noise like a violent, rushing wind, and it filled the whole house where they were sitting. And there appeared to them tongues as of fire distributing themselves, and they rested on each one of them. And they were filled with the Holy

Spirit and began to speak with other tongues, as the Spirit was giving them utterance" (Acts 2:3,4).

Then Peter explained to the crowd that gathered that they were seeing the working of God's Spirit and told them about Jesus. The Christian church began that day with the disciples and the three thousand people who joined them because of the day's events.

We can undertake making disciples of all nations with some degree of success without the baptism in the Holy Spirit, but when we do, we are undertaking a supernatural task with limited power.

It is God's will – it is his commandment – that we be baptized with and continually filled with the Holy Spirit: "Be filled with the Spirit" (Ephesians 5:18). The knowledge and reality of the empowering Spirit enables us to reproduce the works of Jesus. (Excerpts from CBN.org)

So, as I see it, the baptism of the Spirit is given so the believer can receive ministry gifts to aid in his or her service to the lord. The In-filling of the Spirit is to replenish the refreshing required to continue day to day. One has to do with reaching out to others. The other has to do with hearing and fellowshiping with God, so we have direction, purpose, and a clear focus.

Revelation #18… God Wants Us To Know That He Is Working Everything Together For Good.

Why should we trust God, give thanks, pray without ceasing, and follow all the other teachings of Jesus? I would venture to say because of Romans 8:28," And we know that all things work together for good to them that love God, to them who are the called according to his purpose."

God's Will is clearly revealed to those who seek it. However, it is accomplished only in the lives of those that love God and are the called according to his purposes. We also know that God calls everyone to repentance and salvation (John 3:16) The next pre- qualifier is that we love God. You would think that his children love their father. If they do not, it's because they do not know him. In any event, loving God is the prime directive. Jesus said, "And thou shalt love the Lord thy God with all thy heart, and with all thy soul, and with all thy mind, and with all thy strength: this is the first commandment." Mark 12:30.

Revelation # 19… God wants us to practice morality.

"You shall have no other gods before Me," "you shall not make for yourself a carved image," "you shall not take the name of the Lord your God in vain,"

"Remember the Sabbath day, to keep it holy," "Honor your father and your mother," "You shall not murder," "You shall not commit adultery," "You shall not steal," "You shall not bear false witness against your neighbor" and "You shall not covet anything that is your neighbor's." (Exodus Chapter 20).

Revelation #20…It is God's will for his children to practice morality. That's why he gave his children the 10-commandments. The fact that they exist shows us the difference between right and wrong. They were never meant to be a standard by which salvation was attained or denied. They were, instead, designed as a moral compass to guide the child of God along life's path towards his or her destiny.

I am sure you will see even more scriptures that will reveal the "Will of God" for your life as you keep reading the Bible. I have listed some more prominent ones so you can get a feel for what to look for as you read.

So far, we have discovered 20 clear revelations from God through the scriptures that should be active in our lives today. Eighteen of these revelational truths are as follows: See if you can find the other two.

- God's will for our lives is to take dominion over evil and live in such a way as to reveal the image and likeness of God.
- It is God's Will for a man to have a woman at his side.

- God's greatest creation, (Mankind), fell into sin and is now in need of a Savior.
- God loves us & does not want us to perish.
- God wants us to repent and accept Jesus as our Savior so we can live in a relationship with him.
- God wants us to live life with a thankful heart.
- God is worthy of our trust and when we trust in, rely upon and adhere to his voice, he will direct our paths.
- God's "highest will" is to bring us back to where he had originally intended us to be, in his image. Thus, he speaks through the pages of the Bible, letting us know he wants us to set ourselves apart for fellowship with him.
- God wants us to allow the mind of Christ to be in us. This is a voluntary act of humility and servitude to God the Father. It is the only way that we can be highly exalted with Christ.
- God wants his "Peace" to rule or referee in our hearts.
- God wants us to prove what is the good, and perfect will of God.
- God wants us to put on the whole armor of God so the devil can't hurt us.
- God wants us to guard our hearts with all diligence.
- God wants us to pray without ceasing.
- God wants us to have fellowship with him.
- God wants us to seek his kingdom first, above all else in life.
- God wants us to be filled with his Holy Spirit.
- God wants us to know that he is working everything together for good.
- God wants us to practice morality, denying immoral impulses and fleshly desires.

The best way to find God's will for your life is not to ask friends, family, or anyone else. They are not God and often are wrong in their own decisions, which, if I am right, will show up in their lives as a testimony against them.

The best way to know God's will is to ask God in prayer, stay in the Bible and look for direction, correction, and guidance. ***It's all there***. If you start a log of scripture verses and what they specifically meant to you, you will have a history to refer to when you feel lost or confused.

Remember This

All scripture is given by inspiration of God, and is profitable for doctrine, for reproof, for correction, for instruction in righteousness:

II Timothy 3:16

The best way to live in this world is to apply the scriptures and live in them moment by moment. The truth you find in the scriptures will far exceed what this world has to offer.

Hearing The Voice of God

Is God speaking to humanity today? Is anybody listening? If God were speaking to you, what do you think he would be saying? Is it too way out to says, "I am hearing from God"? After all, he is the creator of all things. He is the "Supreme Ruler" of the universe. Why would he want to talk to me? How do you know, for sure, that the voice talking to me is God's voice?

We are left here on planet earth, seemingly all alone to fend for ourselves. It's a make it or break its existence with our future in serious doubt of fruition. Is that how you feel? I used to think and feel like that…like… Why do I exist? Why am I here at this place and this time? Do I have a purpose in life? Or am I just drifting with the masses towards an unknown destiny?

Well… I do not think or feel that way anymore. I was a teenager back then, with very little knowledge or wisdom. It has been over 60 years since I felt lost and alone and without hope.

Things changed when I accepted Jesus as my Lord and Savior. He led me to the Bible and I not only discovered my existence and purpose, but also my destiny. I realized I did not have to walk alone through a world that is less than perfect. I found myself in God.

As I searched, prayed, and sought after truth, I began to hear from God. He started speaking directly to my spirit in ways I never knew were even possible. This divine fellowship between God and me proved to me that it was real and that I was really a "Child of God."

The Witness of The Spirit

Romans 8:16, helped me a lot because it said that God would show Himself to me so I would know that I know that I am in his loving care. "The Spirit itself bears witness with our spirit that we are children of God."

If you are still wondering how the Spirit of God testifies or bears witness, I will try again to explain. There are so many little things at so many different times. I guess the most significant would be answered prayer. When you are praying about a thing, asking for specific results and he brings it into reality, you cannot help but acknowledge that it was his doing.

I have seen the hand of the Lord in my life, moving on my behalf; to deliver me from harm and bless me in ways that were so clearly his work of grace.

Then there's the Bible. You have not lived until you read the scriptures and certain promises seem to leap off the page into your heart. You just know that the Holy Spirit is speaking to you and often it is concerning a specific problem or request. God's counsel and guidance becomes alive as you read.

Channels of Communication

God speaks to us in many different ways. If we are aware of them, we will be more ready to listen. Here are the three most important ways to consider:

- **The Bible**…1st and foremost is the "Holy Scriptures." This is where you discover God. his story, actions, character, and love are all clearly revealed. It is a great source of counsel and wisdom.
- **Divine Unction**… The Holy Spirit will drop a thought or even an answer to a situation directly into your heart. You will have a peace about it and you will just know that you know. This is, for sure, a non-verbal communication.
- **God's Messenger**… God will often send a messenger with a "Word of Truth." The messenger could be the pastor of a church in a sermon, a "Bible Study" teacher, a "Godly Friend", "An Angel" in a dream, "A Vision", and even a "Jack Ass" as in the Old Testament. However, be sure that the message lines up with the knowledge of God. It cannot contradict the truths set forth in the Bible. If it does, it is not from God.

If we desire to hear the voice of God, we must open our hearts. We do not hear with our ears. It is the heart that listens. As "Children of God", our hearts cried out for the living God. He is our Father and friend. It is his hand that guides us, helps us, and delivers us. He is the source of our blessings and very existence.

Many folks do not hear from God because they do not want to know. God, for them, is at arm's length and sought after only in a crisis. Day-to-day involvement with God is not on their agenda. Jesus as Lord is, to them, a slogan, not a lifestyle. This has been true for centuries. Here is what Jesus said back in his earthy days:

"He that hath ears to hear, let him hear." Matthew 11:15 He said this because they were not listening. They did not have their ears attached to their hearts.

You must have ears to hear but your ears need to be attached to your heart…meaning, this is a serious matter and it needs your full attention. You must be willing to take it to heart and act upon it.

There are a few things you can do to make it easier to hear the voice of God. Consider these;

- **Establish a Quiet Time**…In today's self-driven world where everything is fast-paced and rushed, it can be hard to hear from God. Although your goal is to hear his voice in any circumstance. However, you must start somewhere and a quiet time is a good place to meditate on the Word and listen.
- **Stop The Mental Traffic Flow**… The devil tries to keep our minds flowing with needless noise. As long as we are thinking about lots of meaningless things, we will not have the time to listen for the "Still Small Voice" of God. Stop the mind chatter and listen.
- **Focus on God**…Seek him while he may be found. Do not wait for him to come to you. Engage in prayer and ask him to share himself with you. This will shut out everything else and clear the channel between you and God. This action is Biblical.

Hear the words of Jesus as you read…

"Ask, and it shall be given you; seek, and ye shall find; knock, and it shall be opened unto you: For every one that asks receives; and he that seeks finds; and to him that knocks, it shall be opened." Matthew 7:7-8.

Accept God's Will… If we do not want to accept God's will, he most likely will not tell us his will. It is clearly revealed in the Bible. However, he wants to share that with you personally from his heart. *Obedience is the key to hearing God's voice.*

Call Upon The Holy Spirit… We were given the Holy Spirit at our "New Birth" (When we accepted Jesus) It is ok to call upon the Holy Spirit to interpret our prayers, heal our wounds, and help us to hear from God. He was given to us for that purpose.

Learn To Recognize God's Voice…You can recognize his voice among all the other voices coming and going through your mind. It just takes practice. Here is what John, the apostle said:

"Beloved, believe not every spirit, but try the spirits whether they are of God: because many false prophets are gone out into the world." I John 4:1

God wants you to examine every thought because all thoughts are not yours. They also enter your mind from Satan, "The Flesh", and "Other's Expectations" as well as from God. The one to act upon is the one that brings you the most peace. If you feel fear, anxiety, confusion, or guilt, reject it, and cast it out immediately. Do not entertain it.

Be Filled With The Spirit… God wants us to be continually filled with his Holy Spirit. This is a daily, if not moment-by-moment, process. We need to walk in his Spirit, live in his Spirit, and apply all that he reveals to us. Listen to what Paul said to the Ephesians. There's a new song in your future.

"And be not drunk with wine, wherein is excess; but be filled with the Spirit; Speaking to yourselves in psalms and hymns and spiritual songs, singing and making melody in your heart to the Lord; Giving thanks always for all things unto God and the Father in the name of our Lord Jesus Christ;" Ephesians 5:18-20

Being filled is a "Be, Being" action verb… meaning allow God to continually fill you. In other words, one time is not enough. It has to be a steady flow of Holy Ghost power to keep you filled and ready to face the world.

When You Don't Hear His Voice

What happens when you just cannot discern which voice is God's? Sometimes, God wants us to use our minds and search for an answer. He will give us indicators and expect us to draw our own conclusion based upon the knowledge of God already revealed. Here are a few indicators that will help you to know if the voice you are hearing is from God:

- Is what's being said contrary to Biblical truth? If so, it is not God talking to you.
- Is what's being said causing confusion, doubt, or anxiety? If so, it's not from God. God's voice always brings peace and has a tone of love and care.
- Is what's being said putting you under false expectations or oppressing you in any way? If so, it's not from God.
- Do you feel good about doing what is being said? If you are afraid and feel a sense of guilt or if you take part in whatever is being asked of you, it's not of God.

Remember, the devil will always lie to you and suggest that you take part in some sort of immorality. It could be anything from telling a lie to stealing to even sex or murder. His goal is to tear down what God has built up in you.

God's voice, on the other hand, always encourages, builds up, strengthens, and is always in an attitude of peace.

Missing Out Is Not An Option

You should never feel sad about missing the "Voice of God." Hear what the scriptures said: "So shall my word be that goes forth out of my mouth: it shall not return unto me void, but it shall accomplish that which I please, and it shall prosper in the thing whereto I sent it." Isaiah 55:11

God knows who you are, where you are and what you are doing. If he wants to talk to you, you will not miss his Word because he says it will not come back to him void but will accomplish that to which he sends it.

Jesus put it this way, "My sheep hear my voice, and I know them, and they follow Me." **John 10:27** If you are his, you will hear him when he calls.

The shepherd trains the sheep to listen for his voice, among many other voices. That is what the Holy Spirit does when he bears witness with our spirit. He is teaching us to discern the voice of God.

"The steps of a man are ordered by the Lord, And He delights in his way. Though he fall, he shall not be utterly cast down; For the Lord upholds him with His hand." Psalm 37:23-24.

God will order our steps, and even when we blow it, if we are truly trying to do his will, He will lift us up and give us a second chance.

Knowing That You Know Comes From Commitment

"Commit thy works unto the LORD, and thy thoughts shall be established." Proverbs 16:3.

If our thoughts are established, we will know that we know what the will of the Lord is and we will already be in close communication with God, our Father who loves us. Paul tells us in Romans how to commit…

"I beseech (Beg) you therefore, brethren, by the mercies of God, that ye present your bodies a living sacrifice, holy, acceptable unto God, which is your reasonable service. And be not conformed to this world: but be ye transformed by the renewing of your mind, that ye may prove what is that good, and acceptable, and perfect, will of God." Romans 12:1-2

It is so much easier to hear when we are submitted to God and his will for our lives. I can remember a story from the Old Testament about a disobedient prophet. God finally opened the mouth of an Ass and rebuked him. (Numbers 22:28-30) We don't want God to have to speak through an Ass before we will listen. It is better to hear and obey and keep the favor of God on us.

The God Who Speaks

God loves to talk, whereas idols do not speak because God is alive, and idols are not. God himself is known as "The Word", and his speech commands nothing to be everything (John 1:1–3).

"The voice of the Lord is powerful; the voice of the Lord is full of majesty" (Psalm 29:4). When God wants the dead to come to life he said, "Live!" (Ezekiel 16:6), and when Jesus wanted his friend to walk out of the grave, he spoke, "Lazarus, come out" (John 11:43). Even now, Jesus is holding together your molecules with his words (Hebrews 1:3). If Jesus were to stop speaking, you would stop existing.

A Still Small Voice

There is only one place in scripture where God is said to have spoken in a "Still Small Voice," It was to Elijah after his dramatic victory over the prophets of Baal (1 Kings 18:20-40;

God is not confined to a single manner of communicating. Elsewhere in scripture, he is said to communicate through a whirlwind (Job 38:1), to announce his presence by an earthquake (Exodus 19:18), and to speak in a voice that sounds like thunder (1 Samuel 2:10; Job 37:2; Psalm 104:7; John 12:29). In Psalm 77:18

His voice is compared to both thunder and a whirlwind and in Revelation 4:5, we're told that lightning and thunder proceed from the throne in heaven.

Nor is God limited to natural phenomena when he speaks. Throughout the Old Testament, he speaks through his prophets. The common thread in all the prophets is the phrase, "Thus says the Lord." he speaks through the writers of scripture. Most graciously, however, he speaks through his only begotten Son, the Lord Jesus. The writer to the Hebrews opens his letter with this truth:

"Long ago, at many times and in many ways, God spoke to our fathers by the prophets, but in these last days he has spoken to us by his Son, whom he appointed the heir of all things, through whom also he created the world" (Hebrews 1:1–2).

Hebrews 1:1-2 tells us that the voice we are hearing is the voice of Jesus. Hebrews says this…

"Keep your lives free from the love of money and be content with what you have, because God has said, "Never will I leave you; never will I forsake you. So we say with confidence, "The Lord is my helper; I will not be afraid. What can mere mortals do to me? Hebrews 13:5-6 NIV

It is less important to know how God speaks to us than it is to know what we should do with what he said. God speaks most clearly to us in our day through his Word. The more we learn it, the more ready we will be to recognize his voice when he speaks, and the more likely we are to obey what we hear.

Let's summarize so we are all on the same page. Here's some of what we know so far:

- God's Word will find you and accomplish everything he desires.
- We need to be filled with the Holy Spirit continually.
- A "Quiet Time" is a good place to listen for God's voice.
- God is not restricted to a "Still Small Voice.
- We are encouraged to try or test the thoughts that enter our minds.
- The Bible is the life-source of all revelation and knowledge.

- The more we are committed to doing God's will, the easier it will be.
- When we cannot discern the voice of God, we should look for indicators.
- The Spirit of God will bear witness with our spirit that we are his children.
- Don't wait for something to happen. **"Ask, knock, and seek."**

The Best Way Is Always God's Way

CONCLUSION

I hope my seven-step journey has helped you to grow in Christ and to actually achieve the transformation that Paul spoke of in Romans 12:2. I know that shifting a paradigm is difficult. Moving from always being negative to positive in attitude is hard to do. Moving from fear and worry to peace is also very difficult. Some who read this book will probably say that…" you just don't understand". "My life is too complicated." "My past is way too painful." "My…Yada! Yada! Yada!"

God never said life would be easy. Nevertheless, God wants us to have his "Mindset". The fall of man into sin has caused multiple realities, one for every person on earth. Most of these realities are not the mindset of God. They are centered in carnality. (Man's natural thinking) Only our "Free Will" and God's grace can produce a shift from our darkness into the light of God's love.

If you want his will, apply what you have learned on this journey until it becomes your way of thinking and your mindset. The question is, "Are you in touch with reality?" If you think you are, whose reality are you touching? God's reality or man's reality? Most of us will have to be transformed so we can touch God's reality.

So, Let's review. How can we be transformed by the renewing of our minds?

- ***Become A Living Sacrifice*** …by not conforming to this world.
- ***Change Your Thought Life***…by casting down imaginations and evil thoughts that seek refuge in your mind.

- ***Stay In a Continual Attitude of Prayer***…by talking to God about the small things as well as the major ones.
- ***Always Be Thankful***…in all things, not for all things.
- ***Believe That Every Day Is A New Day***…because God has created it just for you.
- ***Guard Your Spirit***…because fiery darts are being tossed your way from evil spirits.
- ***Listen For the Whistle***…because God's Peace will referee, letting you know if you are off sides.

I see this journey as stepping stones to your personal freedom in Christ. It can become the foundation upon which you stand. My goal is to help you to fully realize the potential of actually becoming a, "New Creature," in Christ and thereby fully equipped and ready to do the will of God.

This is "Reality Squared" attaining and enjoying the reality of God, which is far above this world's reality. You can attain this reality. God wants you to seek him so he can bless you with his presence.

Note: God is the only true reality. We seek him that we may find ourselves for we are his creation and his children. If you were to ask me what God's reality looks like, I would tell you that it is the epidemy of Love, the fullness of Joy, the ultimate peace, and full of the rest of the fruit of his Spirit.

How will you know when you have arrived at the reality of God? That is easy… you will be in the experience of God, your heavenly Father. It is there, in his presence, that you will realize your divine destiny and enjoy the blessings of the holy Spirit..

As you walk through your day-by-days, you will know that you are fellowshiping with your creator. He will welcome you with open arms.

May our Lord bless you and enrich you and fill you with his good grace as you apply these truths.

SELECTED CHRISTIAN POETRY BY JOHN MARINELLI, THE AUTHOR

"I AM" There

"I AM" There,
At the end of your broken dreams,
Before the sun rises over your day,
Prior to those tear-filled streams.

"I AM" There,
Down that road of despair,
When all appears to be lost,
And no one seems to care.

"I AM" There,
Over all of life's twists and turns,
When tomorrow is all but gone,
And when you are full of concerns.

"I AM" There,
Sayeth the Lord of Host,
To bring you hope and peace,
And the power of my Holy Ghost.

"I AM" There,
To be sure you make it through,
In the midst of every trial,
To bless your life and deliver you.

"I Am" There

"All power is given unto me in heaven and earth. Go ye therefore and teach all nations, baptizing them in the name of the Father, and of the Son, and of the Holy Ghost: Teaching them to observe all things, whatsoever I have commanded you: and lo, I am with you always, even unto the end of the world." Mathew 28:18-20

The Lord is with us always. He never leaves our side, even when we leave His. In every situation, He is there. It's time to count on His presence and trust in His grace.

Guardian Angel

The Angel of the Lord
Comes with a mighty army,
To fight the enemies of God.

Then he opens our eyes
That we might see the battle
And walk where angels trod.

Our guardian angels
Beholds the very face of God,
Standing there on our behalf.

Our guardian angels
Are ready with God's power,
To quiet evil's awful wrath.

"Take heed that ye despise not one of these little ones; for I say unto you, That in heaven, there angels do always behold the face of my Father, which is in heaven" Mathew 18:10

As God's children, we have guardian angels that watch over us and report back to God. They are ministering spirits especially placed in service to help the saints on their way to glory.

The Angel's Camp

The angel of the Lord
Sets up his camp
Around those that reverence God.

Imagine being there
In the midst of
Where angels trod.

What a joy it is
To know God's protection
And to be in the angel's camp.

It is there that God's children
Are delivered from evil's woe
And led by heaven's lamp.

" The angel of the Lord encamps round about them that fear Him, and delivers them" Psalm 34:7

Deliverance come through reverence and respect for God and a belief that He will be there with His angels to help you in times of trouble.

All Creation Waits

A blue-gray sky
Winks at the dawn,
As the morning light
Sings its glorious song.

Life is flourishing everywhere,
Unaware of what's in store.
The sounds of spring beckons,
In a silent and peaceful roar.

Time marches onward,
Towards the brink of day,
As all of creation waits
For God's children to pray.

It's time to stand up and be counted as a child of God. It's time to pray for peace and deliverance. Creation is waiting.

Don't Worry

Don't worry about tomorrow.
You did that yesterday.
Go on with your life
And remember always to pray.

Ask and it shall be given to you,
But this great truth you already know.
Rejoice and be happy, why? Because…
Your harvest comes from what you sow.

I will say it again and even more,
Until it becomes very very clear.
Tomorrow will take care of itself,
But worry is another word for fear.

Now here's what I want you to do.
Trust in the Lord and be of good cheer.
Drop the worry from your vocabulary
And cast out that demon of fear.

Worry is a sin so stop it. Be of good cheer. It's all up to you. Life is too short to spend it worrying.

Arm's Length

I hold the world at arm's length,
That its choices do not interfere.
While it does its own thing,
I watch and wait over here.

My steps must not go that way,
For it's not where I need to be.
The Lord has shown me the path,
That will lead me to my destiny.

The call to follow sin is strong
And pulls at me now and then.
But I know that way
Is full of sorrow and sin.

I must move on in life
Beyond their beckoning call.
It's the right thing to do,
So I do not stumble or fall.

I will not be swayed or misled
By family, friends or business deal.
Their secret thoughts are not mine,
To consider, to admire or feel.

> So I keep the world at "Arm's Length"
> As I journey through this life.
> My faith in Jesus keeps me strong,
> As I walk in His glorious light.

Arm's length is a good policy. Be sure you stay in the Lord and close to Him. It's the only way to keep sane in such a crazy world.

Clutter

Clutter keeps the mind confused,
As images dance through the night.
Lost among those unimportant thoughts,
Are the dreams that once shined bright.

An endless parade of fear and doubt,
Crowds the mind to destroy our day.
Ever soaring on the wings of the soul,
Until it has formed an evil array.

But clutter is by one's choice,
Of those who dance to its beat.
Better to face imaginations' due
Than to fall into utter defeat.

Set up a filter that keeps out unnecessary thoughts. A good practice is to go by the still waters in your mind and rest there until the flow of life situations becomes manageable.

I Find Myself In God

I find myself in God.
He is my "everything"
I know that He is Lord,
My Life, my Hope, and King.

I find myself in God,
Not the ways of sin.
Nor do I look to others,
To know who I really am.

I find myself in God,
To whom I bow on bended knee.
He alone is my joy and strength
And where I want to be.

You cannot really know yourself unless you first know God. He created you in His images and until you discover Him, you will never find yourself.

The Angels Cry "Holy,"

The Angels cry "Holy,"
While sorrow fills the land.
For God's Judgment Day,
Is to come upon every man.

The Angels cry "Holy,"
While mankind goes astray,
Rejecting the love of God,
To follow his own precarious way.

The Angels cry "Holy,"
Knowing the terror of the Lord,
When all who dwell in sin,
Will suddenly be destroyed.

The Angels cry "Holy,"
Waiting for all things new,
Born of the Holy Spirit,
When God's Judgment is through.

The Angels cry "Holy,"
"Holy is the Lamb,"
Waiting for the children of God,
To join "The Great I AM"

Heaven is waiting for us to join our Savior. What a great day that will be. Are you ready? I am.

Rest My Child

Take your peace and be restored
Then put your faith in Jesus, the Lord
He has provided, your mouth to feed.
From the beginning, He knew your need.

Do not worry, fret or even fear,
for, my child, He is always near.
To bless your soul with love and grace,
To be with you, face to face.

Come, my child, near to His throne.
Do not allow your faith to roam.
For those who will not believe,
Can never find rest in times of need.

His word shall see you through.
His grace He freely gives to you.
That you should rest, your soul to keep,
Forever delivered from unbelief.

Go ahead, rest in the Lord. I dare you. It may be scary at first but it sure feels good when you get use to it.

Winning The Battle

We must use the Word of God
To calm emotions that fray.
For the enemy never sleeps,
Until he has led us astray.

So when your emotions overflow
With feelings like depression and fear.
Know this! If you dwell in that place,
You invite the enemy to draw near.

When your emotions rage
With fiery darts aglow,
Stand in the power of the Lord,
Against its awful woe.

And if you get confused
And lost in the storm,
Put your thoughts on trial,
Rejecting all but heaven born.

You can win the battle
That rages within your soul.
By casting down imaginations,
And breaking Satan's hold.

> Remember to focus on Jesus,
> Holding the world at arm's length.
> Lift up your head above the trial,
> And the Lord will give you strength.

"For the weapons of our warfare are not carnal but mighty, through God, to the pulling down of strongholds: casting down imaginations and every high thing that exalts itself against the knowledge of God, and bringing into captivity every thought to the obedience of Christ." II Corinthians 10:3-5 The battle is in our minds and we win by putting our thoughts on trial and casting out all that oppose the knowledge of God. This is true victory.

Little Prisons

Little prisons await the man with a lustful soul.
Bars of selfishness and pride create dungeons of icy cold.

Prisons of shame and jealousy fill the heart with utter despair.
Bars that separate from God and those that really care.

Stand back! While the doors are tightly closed;
Taking away your life, to wither as a dying rose.

Beware of those little prisons that trap the lustful soul.
Keep yourself free from sin through faith in the Christ of old.

Little prisons need not to be your fate.
It is your choice, Spirit or flesh to date.

"O Foolish Galatians, who hath bewitched you, that ye should not obey the truth, before whose eyes Jesus Christ hath been, evidently set forth, crucified among you? Are you so foolish? Having begun in the Spirit, are you now made perfect in the flesh?

We should always seek to dwell in the Spirit, that we would not emulate the deeds of the flesh. When we fall short, we create "little prisons" that keep us in confusion and away from the blessing of God. It's time to walk in the Spirit and break the prisons that so easily beset us

The Wrestling Match

We wrestle not with flesh and blood,
For man is not our enemy.
Instead, we fight demons in the spirit
That seek to steal our destiny.

But our weapons are not earthly,
Like tanks, guns or bombs.
Instead, we "Plead The Blood"
And shout our victory songs.

So do not wrestle with humanity
Even though evil is there.
Go after Satan, the real enemy
And strip his kingdom bare.

"For though we walk in the flesh, we do not war after the flesh: for the weapons of our warfare are not carnal but mighty, through God, to the pulling down of strongholds; casting down imaginations and every high thing that exalts itself above the knowledge of God, and bring into captivity, every thought to the obedience of Christ." II Corinthians 10: 3-6

Don't fight with other people. Just go about your own business, counting on God to be the avenger. He is the one that holds all the power and strength. If we fight in the flesh, we can fall to strongholds and demons. But standing up in the Spirit and using the name of Jesus, applying the knowledge of God in the situation and casting down every ungodly imagination, will always lead us to victory.

Oh' The Blood

Oh, the blood of Jesus
That washed away my sin.
What a great blessing
To have God as my friend.

This one thing I know for sure,
That when I confess my sin,
His cleansing blood will flow,
And I can walk again with Him.

Oh, the blood of Jesus,
How great a sacrifice for me.
For it was the blood of the Lamb
That healed my soul and set me free.

"If we confess our sins, he is faithful and just to forgive us our sins and to cleanse us from all unrighteousness." I John 1:9

It is the blood of Jesus that is the cleansing agent in forgiveness, acceptance by God and salvation of the soul. Without His blood, there would be no payment for sin. Saint John, in chapter three, says that the wages for sin is death. Jesus paid the price so we could go free to serve God, the Father.

One Man

It was by one man, Adam,
That the world fell into sin.
He chose to disobey God's word
And lost God's Spirit within.

No more walks with God
Through the garden of God's grace.
No more close up and personal
To walk along and talk, face to face.

One man, Adam, gave up
The very nature of God.
Never again to stroll along
Where angels once trod.

Evil now flows through his blood
Where only righteousness was before.
He gave up the Spirit of life
To open up death's awful door.

But one Man, Jesus, came from God
To seek and to save that which was lost.
The life of God in man, once again,
Because He paid sin's incredible cost.

" Therefore, as by one man, sin entered into the world, and death by sin; and so death passed upon all men, for that all have sinned. For as by one man's disobedience, many were made sinners, so by the obedience of one, many shall be made righteous." Romans 5:12 & 19

Adam fell and lost the Spirit of God inside of him because of his disobedience; But Jesus obeyed, did not fall and restored what Adam lost. All die in Adam because of sin but all who believe in Jesus shall live in Christ because of His righteousness.

In The Fullness of Time

In the fullness of time,
Jesus came, made of a woman.
Our Heavenly Father sent Him
Because our adoption was at hand.

He was born under the law,
So He might redeem us from it,
And to receive adoption as sons,
Being children of God, we sit.

We who God made His children,
Have the Spirit of His Son,
Deep within our heart of hearts,
So we can finally become one.

"But when the fullness of time was come, God sent forth his son, made of a woman, made under the law, to redeem them that were under the law, that we might receive the adoption of sons. And because we are sons, God has sent forth the spirit of his son into our hearts, crying, Abba, Father." Galatians 4:4-6

We are the adopted sons of God. We, like no other, have the indwelling presence of the Spirit of His Son, who cries out unto God the Father. If your spirit is not crying out to God, you may want to find out why?

Fragile Flower Red

As a flower in earthen sod,
I bloom for thee, oh God.
To blossom with the turn of spring;
To be to you, a beautiful thing.

I lift my Fragile Flower Red
Upward from my earthen bed;
To draw light from God above,
Strength and peace and joy and love.

As a flower, I bloom for thee
That passersby may stop and see.
Your fragrance and beauty I am,
Flowered in grace as a man.

As a flower in earthen sod,
I bloom for thee, oh God.
Upward, I lift my head,
As a Fragile Flower Red.

"Be not conformed to this world, but be ye transformed, by the renewing of your mind, that ye may prove what is that good and acceptable and perfect will of God."

When we look to God as our source, we blossom, much like a flower that draws light from the sun. When we blossom, like a flower, we display the glory and beauty of our creator to all who care to stop and look. This is our divine providence.

ABOUT THE AUTHOR

Rev. Marinelli is an ordained minister, He has formed and been pastor of one church in Wisconsin and was the pastor of another in Alabama. He has also been a youth minister and evangelism director over the years.

Rev. Marinelli has authored over 30-books that can be viewed on his website:

www.marrinellichristianbooks.com

John is an accomplished Christian poet. He also dabbles in songwriting and writing one act Christian plays. He is the Vice President of Have A Heart For Companion Animals, Inc., a "No Kill" animal welfare organization. He volunteers his time promoting fundraising events for www.haveaheartusa.org.

Rev. Marinelli is now retired from the sales and marketing arena after spending over 40 years in business-to-business and non-profit marketing. He enjoys writing Christian themed books, playing chess, singing karaoke and a retired lifestyle in sunny Florida

For More Info eMail Contact **johnmarinelli@embarqmail.com**

Milton Keynes UK
Ingram Content Group UK Ltd.
UKHW010648010324
438562UK00001B/101